The True Story of a W.W. II Undercover Teenager

by

Agnes Láckovič Daluge and Willard Daluge

EDITED BY GEOFFREY L. SCOTT

To: Lois
Agnes M Daluge

AUTHORS'
Direct
BOOKS

are published by:

AUTHORS' *DIRECT* BOOKS
41 12th Avenue North • Hopkins, Minnesota 55343
Toll-free order #1-800-794-7492

Copyright © December 1998 by Agnes and Willard Daluge

Cover art by Tjody A. Jacobsen and Terry L. Jacobsen.

ISBN: 0-9665887-0-3

AUTHORS'
Direct
BOOKS   Bound Edition / December 1998

Table of Contents

To our children and grandchildren:

Margaret & Wally Plank

Greg & Susi

Wendell & Paula Daluge

April & Jonathan

CHAPTER ONE

SLOVAKIAN CHILDHOOD

I was the straw that broke the camel's back. On March 27, 1928 I was born to Ján and Maria Láckovic. I was the fifth of seven children. My parents and my four siblings had been living with my father's mother in the town of Dolne Dubove, Slovakia. But, with my arrival, the crowded house was now full to bursting. So my parents purchased a small home and property in the nearby village of Paderovce.

My father was Ján Láckovic. He was born on April 30, 1890 in Dolne Dubove. While fighting with the Austro-Hungarian Army on the eastern front in World War I, he was shot in the arm. Gangrene set in. Though he did not lose his arm, all the fingers on his right hand were permanently clenched shut into a sort of fist which made his right arm virtually useless, especially for a farmer. Even worse, he was in nearly constant pain. Nonetheless, he somehow managed to get enough done with the help of my mother, and later my brothers, so that he could eke out a living for his growing family.

Agnes's father and mother, Ján Láckovič and Maria Sedlák Láckovič.

My mother's maiden name was Sedlák. She was born in Malzenice, Hungary on December 6, 1896.

Then there came the seven of us, their children. The first five of us were born in Dolne Dubove; and the last two, Rosa and Stefán, were born in Paderovce. Our birth dates were as follows:

Emilia (Mila) — April 30, 1920
Josef — August, 1922
Ernest — April 20, 1924
Anton (Tono) — May, 1926
Agneša — March 27, 1928
Rosa — July 1, 1930
Štefán (Štefo) — July 7, 1937

Our house in Paderovce was a small, four-room building. It was constructed of brick and clay with a thatched straw roof and clay floors. Windows on the front and one side of the house let in the sun. At night, kerosene lamps gave us a little light. But they were rarely lit for long, since we generally rose with the dawn and went to sleep just after dusk.

Like the walls, the floors were also made of brownish beige colored clay. As I grew older, one of my chores was to help sweep the floor. With eight people coming in and out of that small house, it quickly became worn; and that created dust. So we sprinkled water on it to keep the dust settled. If the floor surface chipped, we repaired it by wetting some clay, kneading it until it got soft, working it into the floor and then smoothing it out. My sister and I often wrote our names or made pretty designs on the floor as we sprinkled the water. The designs would stay for a while, slowly disappearing as the water evaporated or as people walked on them.

While this house may not have seemed like much, it was very sturdy. It was, in fact, so well-built that it is still standing today, nearly 70 years later.

In addition to a kitchen, we had a dining room and my mother and father's bedroom. Soon after we moved in, my father added on another room for storage and for keeping the animals. These included a horse and two goats. This room also had a hole in the middle of its floor, which was deep enough to store vegetables, such as carrots and potatoes, on which we lived during the winter. In the back of our lot was a shed for pigs. We were fortunate enough to have four pigs and of course many piglets later on. We butchered two of these pigs a year to provide meat and lard.

We also had chickens and about forty geese. When the geese were little they could feed on grass. But, in the fall, after the harvesting was done, my brother Tono and I (and years later my sister Rosa and I) walked with the geese for half an hour to a field where they could find food. When they had eaten, we returned home with them. Then, at five o'clock the next morning, we would get up, take them

3

out to the field to feed once more, and then bring them back home by about 8:00 a.m. Around 5:00 in the afternoon, I took them out to the fields again and returned home once more by 8:00 p.m. Tono and I continued this geese-feeding routine throughout the autumn.

Sometimes the geese would get mad, usually when I was moving the flock home or to a different field. Once, a gander attacked me. Unfortunately, my small size and anemic health meant I couldn't move fast enough to get away, and he caught me and bit my hips and buttocks (I still have the scars.) That gander sure had a funny way of thanking me for taking them to dinner!

After that incident, Tono gave me a stick to protect myself. And while I may not have been fast on my feet, I quickly learned how to handle that stick. As fall ended, my mother butchered the geese for the winter.

"Agnes, you have done a wonderful job with these geese. See how big and fat they are," she said, holding up the carcass after the feathers had been plucked.

My older sister Mila and I did not have a bedroom as such. Instead, we slept behind the clay stove which heated the whole house. The "bed" we shared was really just a couple of boards, with wooden pegs underneath to raise it off the floor. A layer of straw covered the boards and on top of the straw was a rough mattress stuffed with goose and chicken feathers. The bed was warm, but bed bugs were a big problem. My mother changed the straw twice a year: once in the spring and again in the fall when the straw was fresh from the fields. Later, after my sister Rosa was born, Mila had to move into the room with my brothers, and Rosa and I shared the sort of simple double bed I just described.

Our eating arrangements were also simple. The whole family, eventually nine of us, would eat at a single table with rough benches on either side of it. In front of each of us were a bowl and a spoon. We had no knives for eating. And, as for forks, well, I never saw one until I went to Germany.

The lack of silverware was no great handicap, because even though we had our own meat, we only ate it once a week – on Sunday. We very seldom baked the meat because this shrank it too much. Instead, Mother usually boiled it, since the water could later be used with vegetables to make a soup. In this way, we made our meat go even further.

I remember one time when we had a chicken and my mother boiled it in a pot of water to make soup. Then she divided the chicken meat among the nine of us. I only got the bottom part of a wing, which had almost no meat. Today chicken wings are appetizers, but, back then, it was my main course! So, naturally, meat served as an entrée was a rare treat for us. Usually we had soups and stews, and, for them, our spoons and bowls were all we needed.

When we butchered pigs, we always smoked them. We smoked sausages, too. Smoking was our main way of preserving meat, because we didn't have refrigerators, freezers or any other appliances. We packed the meat tightly in large clay pots and then poured the meat's grease over the top to seal the pot. If we wanted a cold lunch, we would just slice off the smoked pork or dig it out of one of the pots and then eat it with a piece of bread.

We had a good-sized garden, about 50-feet wide and 300-feet long, which took up most of the open space behind the buildings. The garden had to be that big because it was our main source of food throughout the year, especially during the winter. We also had a variety of fruit trees, including plum, walnut, apple, and pear. They gave us marmalade to spread on our breakfast bread.

Every week, Mother used to bake about ten round loaves of bread in a clay oven my father built for her. During the fall, when we had cabbage, Mother put the leaves from it beneath the bread dough, before it went into the oven. This kept the ashes from sticking to the bottoms of the loaves.

Between the bread oven and the clay stove, we used quite a bit of wood for fuel. So another of my chores was to walk through the forests picking up sticks and branches. Often one of my brothers would help me. Sometimes, when wood was scarce or during a cold snap, we burned dried corn cobs, which provided instant heat.

In Paderovce, only the "wealthy" owned cows. That meant they had butter for cooking and milk for drinking. But families like ours got by with lard from the pigs for cooking. We had eggs, but they weren't fresh eggs. Instead, my mother stored them for the winter in heavy, thick chalk which preserved them for up to four months. Mother then pulled the eggs from the chalk as she needed them. She also preserved pickles and sauerkraut in big barrels.

A couple of pigs, a few chickens and geese, produce from the garden, and fruit from the trees were my family's sustenance during my childhood in

Paderovce. We were pretty much self-sufficient. The only things we bought at the local general store were those that we could not produce or grow for ourselves: salt, sugar, yeast, vinegar, and kerosene. This store was located on the other end of Paderovce, far from our house. But it was an even longer journey when hardware and tools were needed. For those we had to travel about 14 kilometers to a larger town, such as Trnava.

A small brook behind our shed provided water for the animals, as well as our bathing and laundering needs. Most of our neighbors had gardens in the back of their houses, so they also used the brook. Because this brook was used for so many things by a variety of people, it was not clean enough for drinking. So, in the middle of Paderovce, there was a well for drinking water. Just like in the nursery rhyme, one of our daily chores was to fetch pails of water. We turned a crank that lowered a bucket on a rope down into the well. Then we cranked in the other direction to raise the full bucket of water. We then tipped the contents of the bucket into our pail for the walk home. My older brothers and sister could carry two pails, but with my small size and frail health, one pail was the most I could handle. When we got home, the water was poured into one of three covered containers with a ladle. This was our drinking and cooking water. It also served us for brushing our teeth, which we did with our fingers because we didn't have toothbrushes.

In front of our house ran the gravel road that was Paderovce's main street. The traffic on this street was comprised of people on foot or horseback and passengers in horse-drawn carriages, since no one had automobiles. There were, however, buses, which picked up people in the small towns around our area and took them to Trnava, where they could catch trains.

On the other side of the road, opposite our house, my parents had another quarter acre of land. There we stored all of our straw and field equipment, as well as potatoes and beets. The straw provided bedding for the animals and for us.

Our farm was small. My father had three acres of his own and another two acres that he rented. We couldn't afford tools for cultivating and working in the fields. So we had to weed and cultivate our fields just as we did our kitchen garden behind the house – by hand! During the summer, day in and day out, we weeded the fields that way.

Still, as small as it was, our farm produced enough wheat and oats to make flour. After the grain had been harvested by hand using huge scythes, the threshing machines came. These steam-powered machines and their crews went from one farm to another, threshing the grain from the stacks for each farmer. Two men operated the machines, and, since our farm was quite small, it only took them about three to four hours to thresh all of our wheat and oats.

Even so, we always served the workers a lunch of scrambled eggs, as well as sliced cucumbers with cream on them and a dash of paprika for color. Sometimes, when the workers went to several farms in a single day, they were fed so often that they couldn't finish their portions. My sister and I would be right there waiting for them to give us their plates to clean off. And we cleaned them all right – with our tongues!

My mother rarely served us scrambled eggs, so these leftovers were a real treat for us.

Once the threshing was completed, my father took the grain to a mill in a nearby town. The closest mill was in Radocovce, which was about two miles away. My father paid the miller for grinding the grain by letting him keep some of it for himself.

Besides the resulting flour, we also had a mountain of straw to store for the winter. All of that straw was resistible to my siblings and me. We played on the giant mound of it, climbing up and sliding down. We tussled on it and played king-of-the-mountain. When I was about six, I was sliding down such a straw mound and, because we didn't wear panties in Slovakia in those days, a piece of straw went up my butt. It was really painful, and it must have caused an infection because I ran a high fever. My mother tried to dig the straw out with a needle, but, every time, the straw would break off without coming out.

Finally, my condition got so bad that my family took me to the hospital in Trnava. There, the doctors determined that there wasn't much they could do. They feared that, if they cut into the area, they would spread the infection. Finally, they decided that the straw would work its way out over time. But it must have been a dangerous situation, because it was almost two weeks before the doctors let me go home from the hospital. It seemed that I cried the whole time I was there, not only from pain, but from loneliness.

★ ★ ★

In 1935 I started school. It was a small, single-story building about a ten-minute walk from our home. We had just one classroom and one teacher for 30 students in grades one through eight. My first-grade class had six students, four boys and two girls. Our teacher, Mr. Kovacek, lived with his wife in another room of the schoolhouse. In addition to teaching school, he had some medical and first-aid training. He would often help sick or injured people from the town, since the nearest doctor was a three-hour journey on foot to Trnava.

Before school started that year, my parents asked this teacher if he thought I was ready for school. Once he met me, he told my mother and father that he wouldn't let me attend class because I was so small and sick-looking. "She needs to stay home another year and grow some," he told them.

My older brothers and sister, who were already in school, were normal sized and healthy, so he must have thought there was really something wrong with me.

The teacher's answer didn't sit well with my parents. They asked him and then *begged* him to at least let me give school a try. I remember my father arguing with Mr. Kovacek, saying, "Why should you worry, as long as she doesn't die in your arms. She'll die in *my* arms!"

And, while that kind of argument may not have been very persuasive, my parents' stubbornness was – and it won out. Thus, at age seven, I started school.

The classroom consisted mainly of long tables and benches upon which we sat. The layout made it very easy to cheat by copying other students' papers. But, if the teacher caught one of us doing this, the punishment was a hard whack on the back with a stick!

Since I had no shoes, I walked to school barefoot when the weather was warm, and, in the winter, I wrapped rags around my feet. School started each weekday at 8:00 a.m. We began the school day with a prayer, and we were usually done at 4:00 p.m.; although the teacher sometimes kept us longer, if we were behind on our lessons or if we had misbehaved that day. Mainly we studied reading, writing, and arithmetic. Every Wednesday afternoon, the Catholic priest, who served the towns in our area, would come into the school for two hours to teach catechism During that time, the Lutheran or Jewish children would go home or receive their own instruction.

We had an hour for lunch, which usually consisted of bread and soup prepared by the teacher's wife. There was no recess, but, during noon break, we had plenty of time to play all sorts of games. Hopscotch and jump rope were favorites. And sometimes we played "overs," a game in which the boys lined up on one side and the girls on the other and each side tried to get a ball back and forth without dropping it.

Usually, we stuck with children our own age. The older boys were always off by themselves playing football (soccer).

For arithmetic, we copied most of our work off of the blackboard. Because there were so few textbooks, two students shared each book. Many times this meant arguments about who got to take the book home for studying – especially right before a test. The school provided paper and pencils, but that meant that we didn't dare wrinkle the paper or lose a pencil going to or from school, since these things were great luxuries.

That year, out of the six first graders attending my school, the one who the teacher thought would never make it through the classes, was the one who did the best. My parents were proud of me; and the teacher apologized for trying to make me stay home. He said that, the first time he saw me, he thought I was just a little crippled kid and wouldn't be able to do anything.

In addition to the school, Paderovce had a Catholic church that held about forty people. We didn't have church every Sunday because Paderovce was served by a sort of circuit-riding priest – the same one who taught our catechism class. So, if we wanted to go to church every Sunday, we would have had to travel to Bohunice or Radovce or whatever nearby town was hosting mass.

Like all of the other buildings in town, the church was a simple structure. The children sat on the floor by the altar, and the adults sat in the back on benches. The collection of the offering was always interesting. Because Paderovce was a fairly poor town, people would often make their offering "in kind." Instead of giving money, they donated a bag of flour or a chicken. When the priest left town after the service, the back of his little four-wheeled cart looked more like he was going to market than leaving church. Two children would pull it for him; and, more often than not, he would give the produce or poultry to the needy or the Gypsies in the next town on his circuit.

★ ★ ★

In January, 1936, I fell very ill. I don't know what was ailing me, but I was deathly sick for nearly three months. Again I ran a high fever, this time with very bad headaches. Most frightening, though, was what happened to my eyes. My eyelids would stick shut, cemented by a yellow-green matter that dried into a hard crust. As I rubbed and itched my eyes and struggled to open them each morning, I pulled off all of my eyelashes. During the day, I could only keep my eyes open for an hour or so, and then they would be sealed shut again by that yellowish green matter, making me, for all practical purposes, blind.

My teacher, with his first-aid training, told my parents to take me to the hospital in Trnava; but my parents didn't think I would survive the journey.

Then the teacher said, "Well then, you should just give up on her, let her lie down and go to sleep." Of course by "sleep" he meant die.

I also remember hearing at this time that my father's sister, my aunt who lived in Germany, was upset about me and had written asking why my father wasn't doing anything about my condition.

But, most of all, I remember my mother holding me in her arms and telling me that I would get well and that everything would be better. She often had to be away from me because she was needed for the fieldwork. But, when she returned to the house, she would sing me Slovakian folk songs as she held and cuddled me. Songs like *"Jelen sa Pase"* (A Deer is Grazing) and *"Okola Trnava"* (Around Trnava). When I could, I sang along with her. And I remember those songs to this day.

★ ★ ★

By late March, I was somewhat better, but still very weak. So my teacher, who had continued to ask

13

my brothers and sister about me, suggested that I try drinking warm goat's milk to get my strength back. I took my cup and went with my mother twice a day, morning and evening, to milk our goat. Mother milked it right into my cup so I would be able to drink it fresh. Unfortunately, along with fresh goat's milk, I also got fresh goat's *hair* sometimes. I haven't been very fond of goat's milk since then!

My strength did begin to return, but I was still having problems with my eyes. So my teacher told my parents to go to a certain spring nearby, because the water there was supposed to have medicinal properties. After six weeks of drinking the goat's milk, I became strong enough to walk the two miles to fetch the curative water myself. The spring bubbled right up out of the ground. On each visit, I filled up a liter-sized milk can with the cold water and carried it back home with me. I was gone for hours on these trips, and my mother worried; yet she somehow knew I would come back and that I would be all right. I began to wash my eyes with the spring water. I also held a rag dipped in the water on them. It helped. I no longer had to pull my lids open; they started opening on their own once more.

★ ★ ★

By June, I was not only in good health again, but, much to the surprise of my teacher, I had caught up on my school work. The rest of the school year (May and June) went well, and I passed for the year, in spite of my long illness.

My closest friend at that time was a girl named Stefina, who was also eight. She, along with a couple of older neighbor girls, Elana and Maria, thought they were very smart. And, because their families were better off than ours, they would often tease me about having so little by showing off their clothes and toys. It was true that I didn't have much. I wore the same blue and gray print dress day in and day out. It was often as long as four weeks between washings, because we never had much grease with which to make soap; and buying some would have been an unthinkable luxury.

With my poor health and ragged clothes, I think these girls figured that I would not live long. Indeed, it seemed they had me buried already. So why should they have worried about hurting my feelings? I tried not to be bothered by their showing off and teasing. Instead, I concentrated on doing well in school and being as smart as they were. I wasn't so much jealous of their possessions and means, as I was hurt that they couldn't just let me be their friend.

One example of their teasing that I remember best took place on a day when they were making these marvelous finger rings out of wheat stalks. They wove the stalks in and out to create a lovely pattern. I thought these rings were the most beautiful things I had ever seen. For nearly a week, I went over to their homes and admired these rings with the hope that they would teach me how to make one. Oh, I wanted one of those rings in the worst way!

But they never showed me how to make one. Instead, they laughed at me because they could see how much I wanted this information. After the fun of that sort of teasing apparently grew stale for them, they told me that, if I ate some dirt, they would give me one of the rings. I was so desperate that I did what they asked. But they wanted to be sure that I had really eaten the dirt, so they made me open my mouth so they could see that I had actually swallowed some. Only then did they give me the ring.

When I got home, my mother knew something was amiss when she saw the ring. So, when she asked me, I told her exactly how I'd obtained it. She was very embarrassed. "We may be poor," she said, "but not so poor that we have to eat *dirt!*" Many decades later when I returned to visit Paderovce, I looked for Stefina, but she was never home when I stopped by. I often wonder if she felt ashamed for the way she had teased me as a child. Or did she feel that, once I returned as a "rich American" (*all* Americans are rich, after all) the tables would be turned. I never saw her again, so I will never know.

Soon after the dirt-eating incident, however, I made a wonderful new girl friend, a true friend. Her name was Martha Schmidt, and she was the daughter of the Jew who ran the mill in Radocovce. I don't know why Martha liked me, but she was smart and did well in school too, so we had that in common. Also, my father would occasionally take our grain to Mr. Schmidt's mill, so I had an excuse sometimes to visit Martha. My older brother, Josef, desperately wanted to work at Schmidt's mill; but, because of his business dealings with my father, Martha's father knew how poor our family was. I think that is why, even though we were best friends, her parents didn't allow me to visit her very often.

Sometimes, though, she would invite me over and take me in through the back door, so her parents wouldn't know I was there. The house was attached to the mill and, since her parents were often occupied with their business, we could sneak up to her room. I couldn't believe she had her very own bedroom! It seemed to me like a room in a palace. Of course, Martha was an only child, and I was just one of six.

Because Martha's family was better off financially, she was always dressed well. But she was so kind that she gave me some of her old clothes. To her they were old, but to me they were better than anything I'd ever owned. She would also give me some of her old shoes, which were the first shoes I had ever worn. They even fit!

I don't think her parents knew exactly how much she gave me. And my parents never said anything about getting the clothes. When I would wear them to school, the other kids would make a point of teasing me about the fact that they were Martha's. But I didn't care. I was just proud to be wearing such nice things.

★ ★ ★

1936 had been a very difficult year for me due to my long illness and having to work so hard to get caught up in school. And, as the year drew to a close, more troubles arose. Things began to get bad for the Jews living in our area. Lots of the townspeople were against them.

I told my mother, "I can't go to Martha now, because she is a Jew and, if the other people find out, they will make trouble for me."

My mother said, "No, Agneška. You go see Martha, but you see her as a friend, not a Jew." So I continued to visit her.

One afternoon in November, 1936, poor Martha confided in me that the people in the area were no longer coming to her father's mill. "They won't do business with a Jew," she said.

The business was dying, and so her father had decided to move the family that very night. I wanted desperately to be sure I could say good-bye to her when she left. But Martha made me swear not to tell anyone about her family's plans, because there might be trouble if people found out about it. What was more, she didn't want me to be persecuted for divulging such information before the fact.

We both cried, and she left me some of her things which she knew she would not be able to take with her. That very night Martha and her family simply packed everything they could carry and left the mill, their house, and their friends behind. Martha and I promised to write each other, but I never heard from her again. She was my best and truest friend during my years in Paderovce and, to this day, I cannot forget her.

★ ★ ★

During the Christmas/New Year's Holiday that year, a letter came to our house postmarked *"Deutschland"* (Germany.) This was a big event because we so rarely received mail and also because it came from my father's sister, Rosa. She was two years my father's senior, and she was married to a prominent architect in Munich. While reading this letter to our

Agnes's paternal aunt, Rosa Láckovič Schneider.

family, Father finally revealed that Aunt Rosa had been sending him money every month to help with our expenses. Rosa knew that Father's war injury made it difficult for him to support all of us. At the time, I was too young to really comprehend all of this. I only understood that Aunt Rosa was nice to Father and us.

★ ★ ★

As April, 1937 arrived, so did plowing time. My brothers used a single-horse plow in the fields. As often happened during this season, the plow blade got dull, and I was given the task of carrying the blade two miles to have it sharpened at the blacksmith's shop in Dolne Dubove. My sister, Rosa, who was only seven, went with me. It didn't take long to get it sharpened, so we were soon on our way again; but the blade was getting to feel pretty heavy. I had a beautiful handkerchief, which I put in my hand, and I rested the blade on it as we skipped down the dusty road home.

Then, however, I got a little too bold for my own good. I put the blade behind by back, still holding it with my hands, but with the sharp edge down. On the very first skip, my heel kicked up, right onto the sharpened edge of the plow blade. It cut deeply into the back of my foot, and the wound began to bleed very heavily.

So there I was, nine years old (with my seven-year-old sister) quite a distance from home and bleeding like a stuck pig. We weren't sure what to do, so we simply tied the handkerchief around my heel and kept walking. For over a mile I left a trail of blood in the road, all the way home.

Once back in Paderovce, my parents rushed me

once again to the school teacher/first-aid doctor. (By this point, I'm sure I must have been one of his most frequent patients!) He put some salve on the wound and bandaged it. Nevertheless, it soon became infected and I began running a very high fever. It was so bad that even my family didn't think I would live through it. At some point during my illness, my mother put goose grease on the wound, which actually seemed to help. After many weeks, the infection subsided and I finally started to heal.

Something else happened that summer of 1937. My mother gave birth to child number seven, my brother Stefán. A woman in Paderovce acted as a midwife, but my mother's labor was brief, so, by the time the midwife got to our house, my father had delivered Stefán. And, according to what I was told, Father had delivered five of the rest of us as well. Somehow that man, with only one good hand, was still able to deliver his babies!

However short my mother's labor with Stefán, though, I still recall my sisters and I lying in our bed, hearing her moans and screams in childbirth, just on the other side of the thin wall of my parent's bedroom. So I will always remember the summer of 1937 as a painful one!

★ ★ ★

When autumn arrived, my foot had finally healed fully, I had a new baby brother, and I was ready to go back to school. Soon I was at the top of my class once again. But the fall of 1937 was memorable due to more than just academic success. We also helped husk corn in the shed that year. It was a lot of fun. We sang quite a bit while we were doing it, which helped to keep us warm in the process. Then, after the corn had been husked, we tied it in bundles and hung it from the rafters to dry.

On another fun night, we were all sitting at the kitchen table, stripping goose feathers from the quills for pillow stuffing; and I guess we were getting a little wild, because soon the feathers were flying and my brothers were tussling – something we weren't allowed to do in the house. In the middle of all this commotion, my brother Ernest got up and hit the kitchen window with his elbow, breaking it in the process.

The windows weren't very big, but a broken one, especially in November, was not a good thing. Replacing it was an expense our family could ill afford. So, it was immediately clear that the situation was very serious. In lieu of replacing the glass, we stuffed rags into the broken window, and they stayed there all winter. In fact, it wasn't until the spring, that we had enough money to purchase the replacement glass in Trnava.

So, the problem got solved, but on that November night, my Father became as angry as I had ever seen him! He pulled the belt out and made us run between the doors so we each got the belt across our butts. Even though I was the last one through, and I knew he felt sorry for me because of my frequent ailments, he still gave me a lick too, in the obvious interests of treating us all equally.

CHAPTER TWO

AUNT ROSA CALLS

At Christmas time in 1937, another letter arrived from Aunt Rosa in Germany. Although my aunt had lived there for many years she always wrote home in Slovak, so that my father could read her letters. And now I was educated enough to read them, too; and it was very clear that Aunt Rosa was talking about me in this letter. She wrote my father: "I want that sick one, and I will get her well. She is the smartest out of seven, so I want her to come and live with me in Germany."

Well, I didn't know what to think. Would she take me away right then? Would I ever come back to Paderovce? Could I stand being away from my family? What about school? My parents seemed to favor the idea. I'm sure they were thinking that I had been so lucky to survive all of the illnesses and accidents so far, that, if I didn't get some real medical help soon, my luck might run out. We didn't have to decide right then, because Aunt Rosa wrote that she was going to come for a visit that summer.

With the anticipation about seeing Aunt Rosa and wondering if she would really take me to Germany with her, the spring of 1938 flew by. I continued to do well in school. More importantly, however, I managed to avoid any major illnesses. Most of all, though, my mind was fixed on the coming visit of this mysterious woman from Germany.

Aunt Rosa, whose married name was Frau Rosa Schneider, was my father's older sister. She was born in 1888 in Dolne Dubove, the same town in which I was born. But, when Rosa was growing up there, the town was part of the kingdom of Hungary in the Austro-Hungarian Empire, even though its people were Slovakian in speech and culture. As a result, Rosa Láckovič grew up insisting that she was from Hungary, despite the fact that she was every bit as Slovak in her culture and speech as she was Hungarian. I remember later that she often loved to dance the *csardaš*, a Hungarian folk dance. Aunt Rosa seemed to be one of those people who was equally at home in many countries and with many traditions. She *had* to be, with the borders changing so frequently!

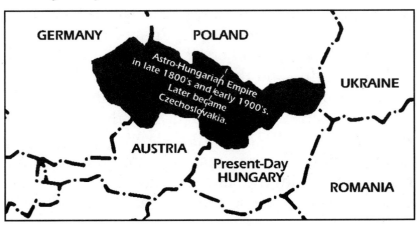

23

Aunt Rosa's personality and character were so forceful that they seemed to open doors for her wherever she went. She had an imposing presence, with a strong build – a trait in our family that I obviously did not inherit. Her face was beautiful, yet it was not a beauty that one attributed so much to her physical features as to what seemed to show from within her.

At 14, she had left Hungary to work as a nanny in Vienna, the capital of the empire. Her experiences changing diapers, she said, forever cured her of the desire to have children of her own. Instead, she later told me, she dreamed of becoming an actress or perhaps a dancer – someone glamorous on the stage, at any rate. Even the movies seemed to intrigue her. She never did achieve this dream, but many years later during W.W. II, her talents and desires in that direction were put to use in a much more demanding role than any part in a stage play or concert could have provided.

In 1912, she married an Austrian named Munk, and together they went to live in Munich, Germany. Munk had started an advertising business; and Aunt Rosa helped him a little with it before the war. But, while her husband was away in the Austro-Hungarian army fighting in World War I, Rosa ran the business by herself. She proved herself to be very independent and resourceful, and the business grew.

Unfortunately, Munk was badly injured in a poison-gas attack and returned from the war in very poor health. In 1922, he died, leaving Aunt Rosa a young widow. But, in typically Aunt Rosa fashion, rather than giving up and resigning herself to a life of widowhood, she charged straight ahead. She kept

Aunt Rosa's Villa Waldeck in St. Margarethen, Germany.

the villa in the small town of St. Margarethen outside Munich where she and Munk had lived. She took in boarders for a time to help provide some income. She continued to go into Munich on the train in an effort to expand her advertising business. With her outgoing, forceful personality she was very successful in making contacts and getting advertising contracts.

Within a couple of years, the business was really thriving, and it demanded so much of her time that she kept the villa mainly for weekends and holidays. Her agency was not the mass-media type we know today. Rather, it was probably something like advertising in the yellow pages or weekly specialized "shopper" supplements. It entailed publishing and distributing a kind of reference book for people, which told them how to find hotels, restaurants, shops, and businesses in Munich. I am sure that, given her aggressive character and love of dances and social events, Rosa made an excellent saleswoman. She soon got to know many of the most important business people in Munich, including many Jews.

This was quite unusual for a woman in this time and place. But my aunt was also quite unusual, especially in her bluntness. For example, I once heard her say about her experience as a nanny, "After that, there's no way I'd wipe anybody's ass!" She would also not hesitate to tell anyone exactly what she thought of them, if she was angry or if the situation demanded it, and even if it meant getting herself in trouble or danger.

Many years later, I remember Aunt Rosa showing me a dance card from one of the many balls that she'd attended during the 1920s. On it was the name of a young Russian student, *Nikita Khruschev!*

In 1925, Aunt Rosa married Herr Schneider, one of the premier architects in Munich. Staying married to someone as willful as my aunt was no small accomplishment. But I think it helped that my uncle was also married to his work. So, this gave my aunt the time and the freedom to pursue her own business and interests. I also think that Uncle understood my aunt's character quite well and knew that a marriage to her would not be particularly "normal."

★ ★ ★

But, getting back to Slovakia in 1938: as often happens, I had built up my aunt's visit to Paderovce so much in my mind, that when she actually arrived, it was something of a disappointment. Aunt Rosa's main reason for returning to her homeland that summer was to visit a local spa named Pieštian. She hoped to get a cure, or at least some relief, for her very painful rheumatoid arthritis. This spa was known throughout Europe and is still extremely popular today, especially for the well-to-do. It was during her stay at Pieštian that she made a day trip by train to Trnava and then by bus to Paderovce. She arrived at our house about 9:30 a.m. and left about 4:00 p.m. to return to Pieštian.

I remember being most impressed by her apparel and her bearing. Though I am sure she wasn't wearing her best clothes for traveling, they were still unlike any others I'd ever seen. She was dressed like an affluent lady; yet she was very approachable and kind.

I heard her trying to convince my parents to send me to stay with her. "Not only will I get Agneška healthy, but you have six others here. Why not let her go?" she asked.

Agnes's Aunt Rosa Schneider, advertising-business owner in Munich, Germany.

As they were conversing, she saw me carrying my infant brother, Štefan around on my back. This was because I was the only one who was big enough and who also had the time to take care of the little guy. Though I was nine years older than Štefan, I wasn't a whole lot bigger. So, as a result of lifting and carrying him so much, I had very bad backaches. Often the pain made me fall as I carried him, but we never seemed to be permanently hurt. I would get up, dust us both off, pick up Štefan again, and continue on my way.

I think that, when Aunt Rosa saw me carrying Štefan around like that, it really strengthened her resolve to bring me to stay with her. She certainly won the argument with my parents, because shortly before she left to catch the bus back to Trnava, she came to me and asked, "Would you like to go to Germany? We can take you to some doctors and try to find out why you are so sickly. Then, when you are healed, you can come back home."

It sounded to me like I would be going just for a summer vacation or maybe a year at the most. But, looking back on it now, I wonder if it was really her intent to have me return home. Maybe she had other things in mind for me even then. In any case, the time away from home sounded both wonderful, and yet sad at the same time. I knew I would miss my family and friends, but spending time with Aunt Rosa seemed like the promise of a great adventure. And I sure didn't want to be sick anymore. So I told her that I would be happy to go to Germany.

"Child," she replied, "that's wonderful. But, first, I want you to finish the next year of school. You look like you are six years old instead of ten. Let's see if you don't grow a little bit. Then, next summer, I'll send you a train ticket and a dress. You can ride the train to Munich, and I will meet you at the station. And we will have a wonderful time together."

By the time of this visit by my aunt, things had already gotten very bad politically. We heard stories of people fighting in the streets elsewhere in Slovakia. Since we did not have any radio or newspapers, we didn't get to hear everything that was going on. So, when we did receive such news, it was often days or even weeks after it happened. Eventually, we learned a lot about what was going on, and it was very puzzling, as well as disturbing. We couldn't imagine people engaging in such violence. My parents said they had never heard or seen anything like it in Slovakia. But then I remembered what had happened to my friend Martha and her parents, and it occurred to me that perhaps this wasn't so unusual after all.

I thought of Martha again on December 6th, St. Nicholas' Day. Thanks to Martha, I finally had a pair of shoes I could shine and leave out for this holiday. Then St. Nicholas would fill them, hopefully, with sweets. Although we didn't have much in the way of actual polish, we used a bit of grease or spit to give our shoes what little shine we could. Then we put them on our windowsill with the hope that St. Nick wouldn't pass us by.

Often someone from the town dressed up like St. Nicholas and another dressed like the devil. They both walked from one end of the town to the other. The devil would be rattling heavy chains, making a loud clanking sound that we heard even inside the house and leaving coal and corn cobs in the shoes of the bad children. But St. Nick was right behind him, chasing him out of town and leaving sweets or other gifts in the good children's shoes.

With my brothers' big shoes in the window, there was just barely enough room for mine. I got a foil-wrapped piece of chocolate, which was an absolutely wonderful treat. This was the only time of year when we got chocolate, so I felt especially lucky, since my brothers got corn cobs!

Then, each year at Christmas, we had a real

Christmas tree with real candles for lights on it. Each of us received a foil-wrapped piece of candy sent from Germany by Aunt Rosa. And, though they did not have our names on them, we knew exactly which candy belonged to which child, because each piece had a picture of a different animal on it. My brothers got the ones with the big animals, like elephants, and my sisters and I got the candy with the pictures of the bunnies or cats on them.

★　★　★

Although Czechoslovakia had already been taken over by the Germans, I don't really recall it happening. I only had a vague sense that the political situation was worsening and people were talking about war. The news continued to reach our family via word of mouth, but, since I was still just a child, it took even longer for me to figure out what was really happening. As I understood things, the Slovaks wanted to remain an independent country, because they used to belong to Hungary. The Poles, however, wanted to overtake Slovakia, and the Germans had their own ideas about what should happen to us. To a ten year old in the remote countryside, it was all pretty confusing, yet I suspect it was hardly less so for many grownups. The main thing, however, was that the adults around us seemed very worried and tense – as though something terrible was about to happen.

★　★　★

Then, in April, 1939, just after my eleventh birthday, my parents let me do something very daring. Thinking back on it now, I'm surprised they agreed to it. But perhaps they thought it might allow me to be healed, which would have eliminated the need to send me to live with Aunt Rosa in Germany. Or, maybe, they were simply preparing me for being away from home; because, until this trip, I never had been – except for my stay in the hospital in Trnava.

Whatever their reasons, however, my parents allowed me to make a pilgrimage to Šastin, a holy place about 25 miles from Paderovce, where miraculous cures were said to have taken place. Aunt Rosa had gone there once as a young woman, prior to moving to Germany. Supposedly it had helped her, so perhaps she was the one who suggested to my parents that they send me there. In any case, Mother and Father were constantly praying for my health, and that had to have been the main reason why they let me go.

Thus I set off one Friday morning, just before Easter, as part of a group of four or five people from Paderovce. We were soon joined by about fifteen other people from surrounding towns who were also making the pilgrimage. But, as we walked along, more and more people from towns along the way joined us; so that, by the time we got to Šastin, there were about 70 of us. When I left home, I took only some bread and eggs with me – not even any salt. Fortunately, another woman named Maria from a nearby town shared some fruit with me. The towns along the way provided water for drinking. Everyone slept outside along the road or wherever they could find a comfortable spot. I was lucky that some nice older women looked out for me on the journey.

We reached Šastin late on Saturday, so we were in time for Sunday Mass. We spent two days and two nights on the grounds around the church building. As we sat, a priest would come out to pray the rosary with us or preach a sermon. All day we would sit and pray for health and healing and for our loved ones. Then, each night, we would simply lie down and sleep in exactly the same spot we'd been in all day.

While I was at Šastin, I received a small rosary with a picture of Mary and the baby Jesus on a small medallion attached to it. I managed to keep it through all of my subsequent adventures during the war, so that, just a few years ago, I was able to pass it on to my granddaughter.

We were fortunate that the weather was sunny and pleasant during this time, although the dryness made the roads very dusty. By the time I returned home, about a week later, the fine dust, almost like beach sand, seemed to have gotten into every pore of my body. And I was so tired that I slept for nearly two days straight. Still, it was a remarkable journey. It's almost unimaginable today that a parent would let his or her 11 year old walk off on such a trip with complete strangers for over a week. But those were very different times, indeed!

★　★　★

As the summer of 1939 began, talk of the coming war was on everyone's lips. Aunt Rosa was becoming very anxious for me to get to Germany quickly. She wrote to my father, "If you don't send that sick one now, it will be too late."

So, in June, Aunt Rosa sent us a train ticket and a dress for me to wear on the trip. This dress was meant to serve two purposes: first, it would make me look presentable when I arrived in Munich, and second, it would help Aunt Rosa identify me in the crowded train station. She assumed that I had grown so much since she'd last seen me, that she wouldn't recognize me. The problem was that she sent a dress that was for an 11 year old, and I was still only the size of a five or six year old. Not only had I not grown since her last visit, I was still under-nourished, had lice in my hair, and my last bath at home had been in *dirty* water! So I assumed that my aunt was in for a rude awakening.

My older sister Mila had been in Munich for several months before this time and had only recently returned to Paderovce. I would later wonder if Aunt Rosa had been sizing Mila up for possible use in her underground activities and concluded that she wasn't suitable – thus her decision to send for me. Or was her invitation to me motivated by something else? With Aunt Rosa one could never tell for sure, as I soon discovered. Nonetheless, it was Mila who left Paderovce with me about noon to take me to the train station at Trnava. There I saw my first railroad train. It was astonishing. I thought it was a monster! I could not believe its size or how much noise it made! The creaking, hissing, crashing, and squealing of its engine and three cars, as it pulled into the station and came to a stop, were so frightening that they took my mind off the fact that I was leaving home indefinitely.

Mila kissed me good-bye and put me on the train and there I sat in my berth with no money to my name. Basically, all I possessed was what Aunt Rosa had sent me: a one-way train ticket and the oversized dress that hung about me like a set of window drapes! In my hand I clutched a little square scarf which held two slices of bread – all the food I had for my trip to Germany. Then, suddenly I heard a crash, a loud hiss of steam and the shouts of some men down on the platform. And, with a sharp jerk or two, the little train pulled out of the station in Trnava, carrying me on the first leg of a journey which would ultimately end ten years and thousands of miles later in Minnesota.

Mila had told me how to change trains in Bratislava and then in Vienna. Because most of the railroad personnel spoke German and I spoke only Slovak, Mila told me to look for a man wearing a certain kind of cap – that of a porter or a conductor. She instructed me to show him my ticket, so he could point me to the right train.

Once in Bratislava, I did indeed spot a man in such a cap, and he graciously showed me the way to the train to Vienna, which turned out to be five or six cars long. Everything – the cities, the railroad stations, and the trains – seemed to be getting bigger and more frightening the farther I got from home.

We reached Vienna about midnight. By then, the noise and the movement of the train were making my head and eyes buzz. Of course, having had nothing more than a slice of bread to eat all day didn't help much either. To make matters worse, it was many hours past my usual bedtime, and I was surrounded by engine noises, electric lights and bustling people. And I knew that somewhere, very far away, my parents and siblings were fast asleep in their beds.

In just a matter of hours, I had not only traveled from the country to the city, but from the 19th to the 20th century. So, it was no wonder my head hurt!

When I got to the platform where the Vienna-to-Munich train was loading, I received another shock. If I was astonished by the size of the train from Bratislava to Vienna, this one positively took my breath away!

"Where does it end?" I asked myself, looking down the 12 cars of the train – not including the engine and coal sections. But, by this time, I was getting pretty good at this train-travel business, so I just lifted the hem of my baggy dress, stepped up into a passenger car, and found my seat. Because it was a night run, there was nothing to eat or drink on the train. And, since the trip from Vienna to Munich took seven hours, I went ahead and ate my second slice of bread. The lights in the passenger cars were turned off soon after we left the station, and I dozed on and off throughout the trip.

About 7:00 a.m., as we prepared to pull into Munich, I looked for a place on the train to at least wash up before I got off to meet Aunt Rosa. But, unfortunately, in my car, there was no washroom. So, Aunt Rosa just had to greet me as I was.

Mila had told me to follow the people getting off my train. "Follow the people, follow the crowd, just keep going with them," she'd said. Luckily, I was smart enough to listen to her. Otherwise, I know I would have become confused and gotten myself turned around and lost

I felt so scared and nervous. I had never seen so many people in one place – and all of them moving, moving, moving. And, again, there was so much noise! There were people shouting to one another and whistles blowing. It seemed like complete chaos to me.

And then I began to worry about what would happen if I didn't find my aunt? But I remembered Mila's words and waded into the flow of people, bobbing along with the throng – and hoping I was headed the right way.

Eventually, I got to the gate where the railroad staff took my ticket on the way off the platform. Just as I handed my ticket over to one of them, I saw a well-dressed lady waving her arm and yelling "Agneška! Agneška!"

I thought to myself, "That's my name, but who is she?" She stood about five-feet ten-inches tall, in a smartly tailored dress and I didn't know her from the man in the moon! She was looking out over the crowd of people, trying to spot someone; yet it was my name she was calling. So I walked over to her, the hem of my dress dragging on the ground all the way.

She was still looking elsewhere when I tugged gently on her skirt and said, "I'm Agneška."

She looked at me for a long moment, and it was as if she'd received a mild electrical shock. She blinked hard and her body twitched for a second. Then the words practically exploded out of her mouth in Slovakian, "Jesus Christ! I thought you were a lot bigger, child. You're sick. We're going right to the hospital!"

After a moment's thought, however, Aunt Rosa must have decided that she couldn't take me to the hospital looking like I did. After all, I was filthy, clad in a very ill-fitting dress, and my hair was greasy and uncombed. I could tell from Aunt Rosa's expression, as she examined my little ponytail, that she had already spotted the lice in my hair.

"No, we can't go to the hospital," she declared. "We will go to a beauty shop first."

"What's a beauty shop?" I asked, having never

heard of such a thing.

She didn't answer. Rather, she placed my hand in hers and marched me briskly off to a shopping area near the train station. As we walked I thought to myself that, if I was about to live in a house that looked as nice as my aunt did, I would surely like it a lot.

At the beauty parlor, they deloused me and cut my hair. And, for the first time in my life, I found myself in a bathtub. Indeed, the beauticians had to scrub with hard-bristled brushes to remove 11 years of Slovakian dust from me!

Aunt Rosa asked one of them to go over to a nearby clothing store and buy me underclothes and a dress my size. In the meantime, I was served a breakfast of rolls with butter and honey. They were so good that I couldn't stop eating. Aunt Rosa sent out again for more bread for me. I just couldn't get enough of it. Then, the beautician returned from the clothing store with several dresses, as well as purses and pairs of shoes, which Aunt Rosa bought for me.

By this time it was nearly noon and Aunt Rosa had a problem. The stores and offices usually closed from 12:00 until about 3:00; so my uncle would be coming home for lunch soon and he expected Aunt Rosa to be there for him. Apparently, she was afraid to take me home without having a doctor examine me first, so she phoned my uncle and told him that I had not arrived yet.

"I am going to have to stay at the train station to wait for her," she fibbed, and, apparently, that was satisfactory with Uncle.

"Child, let's get you to a doctor and see how bad

off you really are," she declared, once she hung up the phone. And, with that, we were on our way again, hand in hand. I remember feeling happy and pleasantly full of breakfast rolls – though still confused by my aunt's conversation with her husband.

The doctor we visited gave me a thorough checkup. When his examination and tests were complete, he told my aunt, "She is so undernourished, this child, that I don't know how she survived. In fact, I don't know whether she will live or not."

"Well, I think she is just hungry and skinny. I am going to feed her and she will be all right," Aunt Rosa shot back.

When I saw how she handled the women in the beauty shop, spoke to my uncle on the phone, and dealt with the doctor, I got my first glimpses of her craftiness, as well as her iron will. I quickly learned that there was much more to Aunt Rosa, than fine clothes and smooth talk.

CHAPTER THREE

MUNICH MORNINGS

As we walked from the doctor's office to Aunt and Uncle's city apartment later that afternoon, I couldn't help gawking at the bustle of Munich all around me. The buildings seemed so tall that I wondered how these people liked living so high in the air. The brick, stone, steel, and huge glass windows of the buildings were a shocking contrast to the thatched straw and packed clay that made up the dwellings in Paderovce. Many times I was looking so intently at the things around me that I nearly stepped off a curb into traffic. So, it was very fortunate that Aunt Rosa kept a firm grip on me!

Naturally, the traffic was also amazing to me. We were in the heart of Munich and the streets were filled with cars, trucks and electric streetcars – the likes of which I had never even seen photographs of in books or magazines. The streetcars were especially intriguing. They had long poles which connected to the wires running above the roadway, and the bursts of sparks they generated, each time they went around corners, were almost magical to me. I had never seen fireworks, so I had nothing to compare them to.

Everywhere I looked there were people, people, people. On my aunt and uncle's street alone it seemed there were as many people as in all of Paderovce.

Aunt Rosa, meanwhile, strode along as though she was oblivious to the fact that I felt as if I were on another planet. She just didn't seem to realize that these sights were stranger to me than anything I could ever have imagined.

We stopped at the foot of the steps of a four-story brick and masonry building, and Aunt Rosa searched her purse for something, eventually pulling out a key. She turned to me and said simply, "This is our apartment building. This is where you will live."

With her key in one hand and my hand in her other, she led me up the steps and into a lobby area. We passed an older couple, who were walking arm

in arm out of the building, and my aunt said something in German to them. The gentleman, in response, touched the brim of his hat in greeting as they passed us. Then I heard Aunt Rosa say something under her breath, once they were out of earshot, and I got the impression that, although she had been

Aunt Rosa's and Uncle Georg's Munich apartment building.

nice to them, she didn't like them very much.

We walked up a flight of stairs to the second floor and down a hall. Then we stopped before a door with a brass handle on it and my aunt used her key to open it. Again in stunning contrast to our house in Paderovce, the apartment had five rooms that were very spacious. Indeed, I was about to discover that I would actually have a whole bedroom to myself. I thought back on my friend Martha's room and I simply couldn't believe my good fortune! Through my aunt's generosity I too not only had nice clothes now, but my own bedroom and my own bed – one I wouldn't have to share with two sisters!

Aunt Rosa had just finished showing me around the apartment, when my uncle came home. I could tell right away when he came in that he was surprised and shocked at the sight of me. I thought it was just seeing me for the first time – a young niece he had never met before – that seemed to take him aback. But he confessed months later, "No, no, Agneška. It was not your presence that surprised me. After all, I had known you were coming for many months. No, I looked so shocked because I could not believe how small and sick-looking you were. I really doubted whether you would live long enough to ever return to Slovakia."

But that day of my arrival he told my aunt, "Rosa, you shouldn't even keep her overnight. You'd better put her in the hospital right away. That child is sick!"

My aunt replied, "Oh, it's all right. I already took her to the doctor and he checked her over. All I need to do is feed her right, and she will be well before you know it."

★ ★ ★

This was Uncle Georg's first marriage and Aunt Rosa's second. They had married when he was thirty nine and she was thirty seven, and they had no children of their own. When I came to Munich in 1939, Uncle was fifty three and Aunt Rosa was fifty one.

Georg was a wonderful man. He was very smart and had a lot of patience with young people. Much more so than my aunt, who was always pushing, push-ing, pushing, with no regard for how young I was. She simply expected me to do what had to be done.

Uncle Georg Schneider, prominent German architect and Rosa's second husband.

It was clear, though, that Aunt Rosa, like my uncle, was concerned not only about my health, but my appearance. For my entire first week in Munich, she wouldn't let me out of the apartment because she was so embarrassed that somebody might see me. It wasn't like I felt confined or caged up, however. On the contrary! I thought I had died and gone to Heaven. I ate like I had never eaten before: bread, meat, potatoes, vegetables and fruit. And, when I wasn't eating, there were so many books, magazines, games, and toys available to me in the apartment that I was busy from the moment I woke up until Aunt turned off my light at bedtime.

★ ★ ★

Within a week's time, the color returned to my cheeks and I began to put on a little weight. Soon Aunt Rosa and I were going for walks in the city and out visiting the staffs of the stores, hotels, and restaurants who were her customers in her advertising business.

What a joy that was for me! I was like a kid in a candy shop. Everything was new and exciting, and I was so impressed with the great, modern way people lived in Munich. I began to fully realize what a limited existence I had had before this time.

★ ★ ★

One of the first places my aunt took me was to see Frau Oswald, a fortuneteller. Frau Oswald foretold people's futures using a deck of Tarot cards, an old method for telling fortunes, which had been popular in Europe for centuries. Depending on which cards turned up and in what sequence, Frau Oswald could, according to her regular customers, tell what was going to happen to them in the future. Like many people of strong will and fiery character, Aunt Rosa was deeply religious, yet also superstitious. For her the line between the two was often rather blurry.

Frau Oswald looked into the future in her very unremarkable apartment, which one entered via a small door that opened off the main corridor of the building. She kept a large poster or sign board advertising her skills in the corner of a window facing the street. It served the double duty of helping people find her and drumming up new business.

As Aunt Rosa and I sat side by side across the table from Frau Oswald, I was intrigued by the colorful and unusual pictures on the Tarot cards. They displayed all sorts of strangely dressed and very old-fashioned-looking people. One by one, Frau Oswald laid out the cards before us on her white linen tablecloth. As she set each one down, face-up, she looked intently at it, then at me, then back at the card.

When she had finished putting out the cards, she waited pensively for a moment, then she spoke in German to Aunt Rosa. "The cards say that, as this child grows older, she will find herself often in great danger. But she will survive the danger and eventually travel a great distance across the ocean. She will marry and have four children."

As my aunt told me in Slovakian what Frau Oswald saw in the cards, I could tell that Rosa was clearly delighted with this "reading" – at least the travel part. At the time I didn't know why, but I think that already she had formed in her mind an ambition for me: that I would someday go to America. She was less than thrilled to hear about the four children, however, since she was not particularly fond of youngsters, especially babies. The strange thing is that, with the exception of the number of children I had – two instead of four – she did indeed give an accurate description of how my life would unfold.

Years later, Aunt Rosa told me that Frau Oswald worked for the Nazis. I couldn't help asking what the Nazis would want with a fortuneteller. Aunt Rosa explained that people would involuntarily tell all sorts of things or betray certain emotions with their expressions, such as fear or anxiety, while the cards were being laid out. Thus Frau Oswald made an excellent informant. Nevertheless, Aunt Rosa believed that Frau Oswald did possess genuine fortunetelling abilities which would reveal that Rosa and I would ultimately be working against the Nazis.

For that reason, my aunt stopped taking me to see her. And, from that point forward, whenever Aunt Rosa would visit her without me, Frau Oswald would ask, "Where's Agnes? What's she up to, learning so many languages and all?"

My aunt would simply reply, "Oh, she's at school or studying with some friends."

Nonetheless, it was clear that Frau Oswald had a vague hunch that I was involved in something which her "employers" would find of interest.

Aunt Rosa's passion for the stage carried over to a deep love for opera, and she soon began taking me to performances at the Munich Opera House. We attended "Carmen," "Der Fliedermaus," and Verdi operas; and I can still recall those afternoons and evenings with her. I watched her face as she stared intently at the stage. She was completely caught up in

the story lines and the beautiful music. Perhaps "diva" could have been added to the list of ambitions that Aunt Rosa held in her heart for herself all of her life. In any case, I know that her passion for opera instilled in me a love for it which I still carry today.

Agnes (left) with Aunt Rosa's maid, autumn of 1939.

45

So, I was certainly allowed to go to the opera and just about everywhere else in Munich back then; yet the one place that was still off limits to me was school. This was primarily because I didn't speak German, but the fact that I was Slovak also posed a problem. This made me an *ausländer* (a foreigner) and this, to the Nazis' way of thinking, meant that I was suspect and undesirable. Thus Aunt Rosa made arrangements for me to begin studying German with a group of Catholic nuns.

Hitler had closed or taken control of many of the Catholic schools in Germany, so I was able to receive instruction from some experienced teachers, who had lost their jobs and were, therefore, quite willing to tutor me. The sisters were, therefore, fairly patient with this, my first, stumbling attempt at learning a foreign language. But they wanted my German to be flawless, so they drilled me and drilled me. When I made a mistake, they would come right to the edge of becoming openly angry with me. Then they'd just as quickly rein themselves in and correct me in very precise detail. They also taught me how to knit and crochet. In both my language studies and my other work, the nuns noticed that, in spite of my own opinion, I was catching on fast.

Although my education in Paderovce wasn't very intensive, I had learned arithmetic not only well, but quickly. I found that that knowledge and those skills helped me greatly in my language work and in everything that would follow. My aunt soon understood that I was quite sharp with memory work, especially in math and languages. Within a few weeks of my arrival, I noticed that she was subtly testing my abilities in these areas. When we were shopping, she asked me about the prices of things that we had looked at or purchased several hours and many stores earlier.

I'd respond with, "You spent 10 pfennigs for that scarf." And I'd be able to tell her the prices of similar items elsewhere in order to help her determine the best buy.

Aunt Rosa later told me that she was very impressed with my ability not only to remember, but to remember specific things in the midst of many other similar things. She referred to this as "my great potential." But potential for what she didn't say.

★ ★ ★

Eating well and regularly did wonders for my health, just as Aunt Rosa had predicted to the doctor the day I arrived in Munich. But there were still problems left over from my malnourished years in Slovakia, which required attention – such as skeletal formation. So Aunt Rosa took me to medical specialists who gave me a regimen of exercises to help me straighten and strengthen my body. My aunt also saw to it that I had special food to keep me strong and healthy. This was not easy because, with the war starting in Poland, many foods were no longer generally available, except on the black market. But Rosa was a real "operator," and, black market or not, she made sure that I had the food the doctors said I needed.

★ ★ ★

One day in late 1939, as we were out on the street, I saw a sight that I had seen almost daily since my arrival in Munich: people walking down the sidewalk with a yellow star pinned to their coats or dresses.

I asked Aunt Rosa, "Who are the people with the stars?"

"Child, let's get back to the apartment. I will tell you all about it there."

I thought it was odd that we had to wait to get home before she would answer me; but, naturally, I didn't question her decision on this. Although a few hours passed before we returned to the apartment, Aunt Rosa had not forgotten my question. We no sooner got our coats off, in fact, when she told me to come and sit beside her on the sofa. When I think back on it now, the explanation she was about to offer was actually the start of the underground work I was to do with her.

"The people with the stars on their coats are Jews. Hitler and his gang, and many others here do not like Jews. So, they make them wear the yellow stars so that they can be identified at a glance on the street or wherever they are. These Jews need our help. What you should know is this: you're 11 years old now, and you have shown me that you have a sharp mind and a quick, accurate memory. You will need those abilities because you are going to have to learn many different languages. That is how you and I will be able to help the Jews and many other people."

"What other people?" I interrupted.

"This war is not going to end soon," Aunt Rosa continued. "Before it is over we are going to have the Americans here. We are going to have the Russians here. Child, it's absolutely essential that you become healthy and get on with your life. We are going to have a lot of work to do."

That "we" sent a chill up my back. But, at the same

time, I also felt a certain surge of pride. This strong woman was including me in what was obviously something very important. Indeed, her air of secrecy regarding the whole issue gave me a feeling that there was danger associated with whatever this work was. Yet, after years of being teased for my small size, ill health, and poor clothing, Aunt Rosa saw me as someone who could be a great help in her work, and this was the best medicine for my spirit.

"Aunt Rosa, are you a Nazi?"

She dropped her voice to a whisper, but the sharpness of her tone was all the more startling for the quietness with which she replied.

"Ptui! God forbid! Hitler, he's the worst of a bad bunch. He and his thugs are bringing war and destruction, not just to Germany but to all of Europe. There is nothing I can do to stop him, but I can do something to help the innocent people who are going to pay the price for his crazed actions. That is the work I do, and that is the work you will be helping me with."

"Why are you whispering?" I asked.

"Because it is very dangerous not to support the Nazis. They have people listening everywhere, even here in our apartment building. If those people hear you say something against the government, the next thing you know you could be in jail. That's why you have to be so careful what you say. For all we know, one of them could be listening outside the apartment door right now. That's also why I have had to be very careful about how much you go out in public. You are not a German; you are an *ausländer*, and so you are automatically an object of suspicion. It is also why it has been difficult to get you into school. Fortunately though, you have picked up enough German very quickly, and, with the help of some people your uncle knows, we will have you in a German school very soon."

"Is Uncle a Nazi? How could you be married to him if he were?"

"No, Uncle is not a Nazi. But he is very well known. One of the top architects in all of Munich. But, since the government controls most of the building projects, Uncle has to be able to work with the Nazis. He doesn't like it very much, but he has little choice. Even so, it is very, very important that you tell him nothing about any work you may be doing with me, unless I say that it is all right. In fact, you must not say anything to anyone about what we are doing. Not friends, not teachers, not policemen, not anyone."

"What happens if I do?"

"You will put yourself and many other people, including me, in great danger. But, until you learn some more languages and have more schooling and get your health completely back, you won't need to worry about those things. For now, you just concentrate on doing the best you can in school," she concluded.

Well that was perfectly fine with me. Aunt Rosa's talk had made me both excited and really nervous. I didn't know much more than I had before, except that Aunt Rosa was involved in something very dangerous and that, eventually, she expected me to help her. As I said, it made me feel important to be included, but I was having such a wonderful time just being in Munich, that I wasn't too sad to hear that, for the time being anyway, I would simply be doing what any nor-mal, 11-year-old girl would.

★ ★ ★

Within a few weeks, Aunt Rosa's prediction about my uncle being able to help get me into a German school came true. In the autumn of 1939, I started attending the Tumblinger School in Munich. Although, at my age, I should have been in the fourth or possibly the fifth grade, I was placed in a second-grade class. I suppose this was because my German was not good enough yet, and maybe it was also because of my being an *ausländer*.

The lady teacher I had was a very dedicated Nazi. She was really mean to me, and she was always telling the other teachers that I didn't belong in the school.

"That one should be working in a factory, not get-ting smart. She is an *ausländer*, you know!" she told my aunt (who, though married to a German, was also an *ausländer* by birth).

The Tumblinger School was one mile from our apartment. There was a shortcut to it, which saved me a couple of blocks of walking. Unfortunately, however, it led right through a cemetery! And what made it even more frightening was that this path ran only about 100-feet away from the mortuary. Unlike the United States where we have funeral homes for view-ing the dead, European cemeteries often have places right in them where family and friends come to see their deceased loved ones before they're buried. Thus, in the cemetery I walked through, the corpses were lined up in a single row, perpendicular to the path. Their coffins or caskets stood almost perfectly upright, just tilted backwards far enough to keep the bodies from pitching forward. Some of the dead had their eyes and mouths wide open in expressions of perpetual surprise. Others had their eyes and mouths only partially open, giving them a downward-looking appearance, as if they were talking quietly to themselves while working through a knotty problem. The eerie sense I got that these people were still alive, but frozen in a particular pose, was emphasized by the lighting from above which cast deep and peculiar shadows under the corpses' eyes and noses.

Taking this route *to* school was not so bad because, when I was headed in that direction, the backs of the coffins were in front of me, so I couldn't see the faces of the dead, unless I turned around to look at them. (Even so, I ran as fast as I could to get to the point where the mortuary was out of sight.) But coming home *from* school was a different story. When walking in that direction, I was facing the dead people for the few minutes it took me to get past them. I tried closing my eyes once, but I found myself wandering off the path, and, with a rush of panic, it occurred to me that this measure might cause me to again go astray and stumble right into one of the caskets! In the end, this "short cut" proved so unnerving to me that I only made use of it when I was late for school or if it was very cold. In either case, I moved as quickly as I could!

On a brighter note, however, I did very well in my studies that year and I was quickly moved into the third grade. Indeed, by the end of 1939, I was speaking German so well that I was able to go into my regular grade.

But, as the war progressed, the Nazis became even

more suspicious of *ausländers*. People like my teacher, who distrusted and hated those (even children) who weren't German, created such a controversy that I was not able to return to the Tumblinger School after the 1939 Christmas holiday.

This upset my aunt very, very much. So she had Uncle use some of his Nazi contacts to get me in-home tutoring, as well as to arrange for me to spend some time in various schools around Munich. He even had an SS man escort me into the schools, so that the teachers wouldn't know I was an *ausländer*. This method worked very well, and no one ever questioned whether I should be in those classrooms.

CHAPTER FOUR

FOUR LANGUAGES IN THREE YEARS

1940 started well. I was enjoying school. My German continued to improve, and I was learning many things which I knew I would never have been taught back in Paderovce. The magic of living in the big city still hadn't worn off for me. Every turn of a corner seemed to present some new marvel – a beautiful church I had never seen before or a shop window filled with marvelous toys, candies or baked goods.

For my twelfth birthday, March 27, 1940, my aunt and uncle gave me a train and boat ticket, so that I could travel to London, England when school was out on July 15th. They told me that I would soon be meeting another private instructor, who would be my companion on the trip and who was to help me learn my third language in addition to Slovak and German: English.

At the end of April, however, the stretch of good health that I'd been enjoying since arriving in Munich, came to a halt. I suddenly fell quite ill with a high fever and painful headaches. The doctor's diagnosis was tonsillitis. He made me spend a few days in bed until the fever broke. Then, several days later, I went back to him to get my tonsils removed.

At his office, I was told to sit in what looked like a dentist's chair. A nurse gave me a shot in the arm, which I think was supposed to put me to sleep. If that was its purpose, however, it didn't work. In fact, I was completely aware of my hands being tied to the arms of the chair minutes later. Then the nurse held a bowl under my chin, and the operation started. I know that I did a lot of screaming, but how long the operation went on, I couldn't say. It seemed like forever!

When the doctor was done, the nurse made sure I looked at the tonsils, for some reason. I saw all that bloody mess in the bowl she held and I promptly passed out.

When I regained consciousness, Aunt Rosa was standing by me with tears pouring down her cheeks. It was the first time I had seen her cry. She had struck me as such a strong woman that these tears surprised me out of dwelling on my own painful predicament. As she stood at my bedside, the doctor gave her instructions on aiding my recovery. He said I should eat ice cream and liquids and that I should spend the next several days in bed.

By the fourth day after the operation, I was feeling much better and I found myself able to eat soup and soft foods. Within a week I was attending classes again, and I finished the school year without further incident.

★　★　★

On July 16th my tutor and I left for London and we arrived there about three days later. I don't remember our exact itinerary, but it seems to me that we went through Italy and Spain or Portugal, then on to London – rather than taking the more common route through France or the low countries of Belgium and the Netherlands. I know that our boat trip to England lasted a day or two, so we did not cross the English Channel.

Germany had just invaded France and the war was spreading throughout Western Europe. So this probably explains why we took the roundabout route. But, to add to my confusion at this point, there was something rather peculiar about my traveling companion. Throughout the trip to England, she hardly ever let me out of her sight. She was very quiet and rarely said or did anything that did not seem like she had carefully thought it through first. As if to add to this woman's air of mystery, I cannot, for the life of me, remember her name today. Although we traveled and lived together for several months, I simply *cannot* recall her name!

When we reached London, my teacher and I lived in a hotel in the London area. I believe that we were in a northwest suburb of London. It is hard for me to be sure of this, however, because it was such a big city and we did not travel much, except for trips between the hotel and my school and the local park. I remember that the park had a pool with a statue which spit water, and my teacher would sit on a nearby bench while I ran about and played.

I was afraid to talk in school sometimes because my English was not very good and I thought the other children would tease me about it. So I found it was easier to make friends and get along when we weren't in class, but were all just playing.

Our daily routine in England was quite simple: at seven-thirty each morning we went down to the hotel dining room for breakfast. The dining room was really more like a large living room filled with small round tables, which were draped with white linen cloths. For long-term guests, such as my tutor and me, the managers placed a card with our names on the same table every day, so that it was reserved for us. My teacher made me sit with my back to the window which faced the street. She said that I kept craning my neck to see what was going on outside and that this was very unbecoming behavior in a young lady. So she took the chair with the view of the street. And, while she didn't actually crane her neck, I could see, from where she was focusing her eyes, that she also didn't miss much that was going on out there.

After a breakfast of hard crescent rolls, butter, honey, marmalade and coffee with milk, we would return to our room to spend most of the morning in private English lessons. I remember that it was a simple room with just one small bed which my teacher and I had to share. Thank goodness we were both so small!

All of our conversation was in English during these lessons. I only reverted to German when I absolutely couldn't understand or say something in English. Teacher loved to talk at length about the King and Queen of England. Thus many of my lessons and language practice had to do with the English royalty. Aunt Rosa, too, was very infatuated with the idea of royalty, having grown up during the reign of the last Hapsburg emperor. So I am sure that this shared interest in royalty had helped cement a bond between my teacher and Aunt Rosa back in Germany.

I also attended an English school for a half a day each week. This was so that I had the opportunity to be with other children and, I suppose, to practice my English with them. In addition to this, my tutor told me that she wanted me to have a chance to see how English children learned. Well, I suppose I did that, but what I most remember are the many wonderful times I had playing games out on their school playground. However, if my teacher's idea was also to help me learn English, these half-days at the English school were a great idea. I know that my English became improved much faster than it would have without them. And I met many new friends to boot. But even on the playground, as was true throughout the whole trip, my teacher virtually never let me out of her sight. It seemed less strange to me then than it does now. At the time, as a youngster of 12 in a strange country, it was probably quite reassuring. But, looking back on it, I have this nagging feeling that there was more going on around me than I realized.

For example, in our hotel room, my teacher sent notes and letters out every day. But we did not post them ourselves or leave them at the front desk when we left, as we saw many of the other residents do. Instead, a uniformed young man would always come up to the room to collect them from her personally. At the time, I assumed he was a bellboy employed by the hotel. But now I'm not so sure. My teacher seemed to know him. She was on quite friendly terms with him, in any case; and they would often spend some time talking quietly at the door. I wasn't able to overhear what they were saying, and I doubt my English would have been good enough to follow their conversation, even if I had.

Nonetheless, I never asked any questions. Aunt Rosa's teachings in that department had already sunk in well. And, besides, I was having a wonderful time in England. I don't even recall anything about the German bombing and the Battle of Britain that were going on at that point. Even so, that daily scene with the letters, coupled with my teacher's constantly hovering presence, seem, in retrospect, slightly odd. Thinking about it today, it's as if I was looking at a picture and I had a nagging feeling that something was missing or that something was going on in the picture that I couldn't quite see. But, at the time, I was enjoying myself tremendously. And, in the process, I had learned yet another language.

★ ★ ★

In November of 1940, one of my back teeth began to ache quite badly. I think my teacher became concerned about what to do with me because I was crying a lot from the pain and could hardly eat. Since our stay in England was almost over, she contacted Aunt Rosa to tell her about my condition and to ask what she should do. Aunt Rosa decided that we should return to Germany immediately, so we went back as soon as we could book passage.

The traveling only worsened my condition, however. Once I was back in Munich, my tooth was throbbing unbearably, so Aunt Rosa took me straight to the dentist. He took one look at the tooth in question and saw that it had a hole in the middle of it and the gum was growing up into the hole and spreading out over the tooth. He told my aunt it was a real mess. He would have to cut the flesh off of the tooth first, just so he could see what he was doing when he pulled it. And all of this would have to be done *without* anesthetic, since it was in such short supply, due to the war. He cut the flesh with a scalpel, which hurt quite a bit, but the bleeding scared me more. Then, the next thing I knew, he was coming at me with a pair of what looked like industrial-strength pliers!

I was still hurting from the incisions, and, when I saw those pliers, I was scared to death! I wanted to get out of the chair and run as far and as fast as I could; but the dentist's assistant, who was not a nurse, pushed down on my shoulders and pinned me there. The dentist, in turn, put his knee on my legs to hold me down more tightly. Then came the huge pliers, which filled my mouth to the point of gagging me. The dentist latched onto the tooth and tugged until I thought my head would snap off my neck! Then, finally, the meaty tooth popped out, and blood sprayed all over me, the dentist and the immediate vicinity.

Needless to say, the pain was absolutely excruciating. Even so, I remember looking, with a certain detached fascination, at the bloody pliers with the tooth still in their grip. "So that came from *my* mouth?" I remember thinking.

Fortunately, however, everything healed quickly, and, by the time Christmas, 1940 arrived, I was ready to enjoy the holiday.

★ ★ ★

We celebrated Christmas in Munich that year, but Aunt and Uncle decided that we would spend the

Degerndorf - St. Margarethen and the Wendelstein Mountains.

New Year in the country. Aunt Rosa and her first husband had owned a large house, a villa really, just outside a small village called St. Margarethen, about 50 kilometers southeast of Munich. When her first husband died, my aunt took in boarders to help meet her expenses. Then, a few years later, she married the prominent Munich architect, Georg Schneider; but she kept the villa, which was named Villa Waldeck. She loved its rural setting on the corner of the forest in the foothills of the Bavarian Alps. She and Uncle used it mainly on weekends and for vacations. The rest of the time they lived in their apartment in Munich. But, once the Allied bombings began, it was safer to be in the country, and the Villa Waldeck eventually became our home.

It took an hour and a half train ride from Munich to Brannenburg, with an intermediate stop in

61

The road that led up the foothills to the villa

Rosenheim, to reach these Bavarian foothills. Then we had to walk for about 30 minutes to finally reach the villa. Ten minutes of this walking was on relatively flat ground, but the last 20 minutes were all up hill! We always traveled on foot in the country, as did our neighbors. And, if we had to carry groceries or parcels from the Brannenburg train station to St. Margarethen, we used a little four-wheeled multi-purpose wagon to haul the load. The only luggage we used to carry our clothes from Munich were rucksacks, which could be carried on ones back. They were the preferred baggage in Germany at that time, whether one was a farmer or an architect.

Villa Waldeck looked like a small hotel. It had ten bedrooms on the upper two floors, while the first floor had a kitchen, large pantry, adjoining winter and summer living rooms and a spacious verandah with a beautiful view. Next to the villa itself was a small, two-room house for the servants, which contained a combination kitchen and living room, as well as a bedroom and a full basement.

Before I arrived, Aunt Rosa kept servants at the villa. But they left just before the war started. When Munich began to be bombed, several years into the war, the government forced Aunt Rosa to let a couple, who had been bombed out of their home, live in the servants' house. By this time, my aunt was using the villa for some of her espionage activities; but she had an almost infallible instinct for knowing whom she could trust and whom she couldn't, and she felt these people wouldn't report her activities to the Nazis. Fortunately, she was correct about them and they never made any trouble for her. In time, however, the servants' house became too small for them and they moved out. After that, Aunt Rosa, determined to keep the little house empty, began to make up excuses for the authorities as to why it couldn't be used to house other bombed-out citizens.

The Villa Waldeck

There was no running water in the villa's rooms, so sanitary facilities were very simple. On the main floor, the bathroom contained only a sink and a bathtub. A second bathroom had just a sink and a toilet. On the upper floors, there were no toilets. Each room had a wash basin and a water pitcher for cleaning up, as well as a chamber pot for going to the bathroom.

Our water supply came from a natural pool, which was located up the mountain behind the villa. A pipe running down from this pool carried water to us. But, contrary to what is thought of as "clear mountain water," this was, by no means, clean. It was full of organisms and even runoff from nearby fields and meadows. And this meant that we had to boil any water that we planned to drink or use in cooking.

A Munich doctor once told us the story of a woman who had taken a drink from a mountain stream in the area. Sometime later, she began to think she was pregnant because her abdomen began to bulge and she felt movement within it. When she went to consult with a doctor, he could find no sign of pregnancy, but did notice that her abdomen was distended. Further tests and, eventually, an operation showed that she had swallowed a snake egg that had been floating in the mountain stream and that somehow that egg had hatched and she, in fact, had a snake growing inside her stomach!

The doctor claimed the story was true and that he had seen the pictures of the operation. Well, whether it was true or not, it was indicative of the "quality" of the water which came into the villa.

★ ★ ★

Each room in the villa was equipped with a tile stove in one of its corners. Aunt Rosa was very frugal, so we used whatever fuel was cheapest. Sometimes we burned coal, but often we used wood from the nearby forests. We also used paper and other scrap material as fuel for these stoves. And, even though the bedrooms were quite large, it didn't take more than an hour of burning to warm them completely.

The two upper floors each had balconies, and the first floor had a spacious, 18-by-50-foot, three-season porch or verandah. It ran nearly the width of the front of the house and it faced down the hill, toward Degerndorf. Sitting on the verandah, one could see a beautiful view of the mountains and the towns spread out across the valley of the River Inn.

The basement of the villa contained a large beer and wine cellar, a laundry room, and a chamber in which we stored the coal, which was used to heat the main floor in the winter. The basement also had a corridor that ran about thirty feet long to a special room, which extended underground beyond the house. My aunt had asked my uncle to build it, apparently as an air-raid shelter.

The kitchen stove contained a big oven, so, after dinner each night during the cold months, we heated bricks in it. Then, at bedtime, we each took a hot brick from the oven, wrapped it in a towel or cloth, and took it upstairs to put in our beds. There were thick pads of soft sheep's wool over our mattresses and feather quilts to pull over of us. Thus the bricks had our bed linens heated in just minutes.

The combination of Villa Waldeck's warm, cozy atmosphere, its breathtaking views, and its proximity to the mountains (where we could picnic, ski and hike) made it my favorite place in Germany.

Indeed, the mountains were at our very doorstep. Wendelstein, one of the highest peaks in the Bavarian Alps, was about an hour's ride up the cog railway from St. Margarethen. The cogs were special gears placed in the center of the normal rail tracks. The cog-rail engine used a geared wheel that meshed with gear teeth in the middle of the rails. This provided enough purchase to allow the train to climb the steep mountain grades.

★ ★ ★

My Christmas presents that year were a pair of skis and a sled. I quickly put them to use when we left Munich the next day to spend the rest of the Christmas and New Year's holidays at the Villa Waldeck. I took skiing lessons from an excellent instructor named Georg, who lived in the village. (Who could have guessed that, over forty years later, Georg would also teach my husband Willard and

Cog-rail train in the foothills of St. Margarethen

our son Wendell to ski!) In any case, this instructor accompanied us to the villa and was great fun to play with out in the snow. But, much as I wanted to, I couldn't spend all my time skiing, because I still had German and math homework to do.

Our next-door neighbor at the Villa Waldeck was an Englishwoman named Professor Sauter. She was a teacher who had married a German man. After his death, she decided to stay in Germany, rather than returning to her native London. Now, with Germany at war with Great Britain, she lived in constant fear that the German authorities were going to force her to return to her homeland. They did not, however. Rather, she died in St. Margarethen, before the war ended.

Aunt Rosa had not liked Professor Sauter when they first became acquainted. But their relationship had improved over the years, and now, when we were at the villa, my aunt took me to her house to practice my English with her. It was typical of Aunt Rosa to not have the time of day for someone until he or she could be of use to her. Thus, even after I began to go to the professor regularly for instruction, Aunt Rosa would imitate her, making fun of her buck teeth and her English accent.

"Nawh, you go offah to Professah Sawtah's," she would say sticking her front teeth over her lower lip. And it was so comical that I couldn't help but laugh.

Professor Sauter (she hated being called "Frau") told my aunt how surprised she was that I had learned English so well in such a short time. "That child must really have a gift for languages," she said. And, during that year's Christmas vacation, I visited her almost every day to speak and read English with her.

She gave me many books to read, including the story of LITTLE RED RIDING HOOD, written in several different languages. I would then read and translate the books or stories she gave me; and, when I was done, I carried over or mailed to her a book report which I wrote in English. This proved an excellent way to make me even more fluent in it.

★　★　★

It seemed we had only just returned to the apartment in Munich at the end of the holidays, when I was whisked away with yet another language teacher to Paris. It was late January 1941, and the train trip we took would lead me to learn my fourth language – French.

Unlike my stay in a hotel in London, our time in Paris was spent in a private home, living with a family which I think must have been the relatives or close friends of my French teacher. But we no sooner arrived in Paris, when my instructor and I made a trip to Switzerland. We went there to visit a couple for whom I had a message from Aunt Rosa. I told them that Aunt Rosa was sorry that she couldn't come to visit them herself, but that she had sent me in her stead. I went on to say that she conveyed her greetings and wishes for their good health. It seemed odd to have me travel so far to deliver such a simple message; but, as I was to I realize later, Aunt Rosa was using me, even then, to convey secret messages. In this case, however, it was to people *outside* of Germany.

With this done, we promptly returned to Paris. The family we were staying with had two children, who were both about my age. My French teacher was very good to me, encouraging me to play with the kids, as well as other youngsters in Paris. I think this was because she knew that I had spent so much of my recent life only in the company of adults and she felt a bit sorry for me. But this lenience on her part was probably a risk for her, since I'm sure it went against my aunt's instructions. Aunt Rosa was only concerned that I work hard and learn French during this stay. And I probably, unwittingly, got my teacher in trouble with my aunt, when, upon returning to Munich, I mentioned to her the wonderful times I'd had playing with the kids in Paris.

Unfortunately, French was more difficult for me than the other languages I'd learned. This was probably because it was the first Romance language (or at least non-Germanic language) I had tried to master. In addition to my language study, I took ballet lessons and learned tumbling at this time. These physical activities helped me to grow stronger and gain some stamina. During my time in Paris, I felt like I was really living fully for this first time. I was so involved with everything: my studies, my new friends, the beautiful buildings and museums, that I didn't notice that Paris was a German-occupied city. My five months there simply sped by.

Immediately upon my return to Munich, we went to the Villa Waldeck for the month of July 1941. As I spent that first night in my second-floor room, I realized how much I'd enjoyed being with other children during my stay in Paris and how much I missed them now. It was a very lonely month for me.

It was also very busy, because my aunt brought four different language teachers to stay with us at the villa. It was her way of thanking them for teaching me: a sort of free vacation in the mountains.

My uncle was concerned that one of them might be a Nazi and would become suspicious about why I was being trained so intensively in so many languages.

Uncle continually warned Aunt Rosa, "Be careful! Don't say anything to them!" But my aunt's instinct for knowing whom she could trust continued to serve her well and no problems came of the instructors' little "vacation."

It wasn't completely a vacation for them, however. They did work a bit with me. Each day I studied with a different teacher in a rotation: Wednesdays were for German, Thursdays for French, Fridays for English and so on. This was easy for the teachers, because they had three days off for every one on. But, for me, it was a month of constant, intense study – and in a different language every day. And, to make matters worse, this work seemed doubly hard after the wonderful, unregimented months I'd just enjoyed in France. Thus, I was very glad to see July finally come to an end!

My uncle, though a very quiet and private man, was also sensitive to my moods. He must have noticed my loneliness, because he said to my aunt, "I wonder why Agnes looks so sad. It's not good for a child to look that way. She needs to perk up. And Rosa, she's not eating as well as she did a year ago. She's not growing much. What could be wrong? Maybe she should be more with children instead of us grownups?"

My uncle had deduced my problem exactly, and this, in turn, gave my aunt an idea: Perhaps it would help me to have visitors from Slovakia. Thus, she sent two train tickets home to my two sisters, Rosa and

Mila, so they could come to stay with me for two weeks at the end of August. Well, the two weeks turned into *years*, as both of my sisters decided to stay in Germany and get jobs when they were old enough. My older sister, Mila, began working as a housemaid for two of my aunt's friends, a husband and wife who

were both professors living in a northern suburb of Munich. And my little sister, Rosa, stayed with us and was able to go to a German school on a part-time basis, as well as having a teacher come to the house. Rosa and Mila both loved Munich, just as I did. For the first time, they were assured of having plenty of food, clothing, and shoes. It was such a big change for the better from Paderovce.

Agnes with her bicycle near orchard, underneath which was Rosa's secret, basement room for people fleeing the Nazis.

Of course my mother and father were very sad that the girls had left home. Since my older brother, Josef, had already joined the military in Slovakia, half of their children had, by this time, "left the nest." And, because my parents now had fewer mouths to feed, Aunt Rosa no longer saw reason to send my father the one-hundred marks a month. But Mila was getting one-hundred marks per month, so she was able to send eighty of them home to our parents instead.

She could send so much home because the professors she worked for were very good to her, giving her almost everything she needed, so she didn't need to buy much.

She used to say to me, "Just think, Agneška, I'm living in a warm house with my own room on the second floor. And three good meals every day. What more could I want? And no more sprinkling the clay floors and sweeping them," she'd add, laughing. "Compared to home, working for the professors is so easy!"

Nearly every Sunday afternoon, my sister Rosa and I visited Mila. It was a forty-five-minute streetcar ride. The professors always welcomed us and told Mila to make us coffee and give us cake or whatever they were serving that day.

★ ★ ★

In October, 1941 my uncle remarked to Aunt Rosa, "Do you see how happy Agnes looks? The color has come back into her cheeks. It was a good idea to bring her sisters here."

"I told you, two piggies eat better than one," my aunt replied.

★ ★ ★

For some time my aunt had been mentioning little bits and pieces to me about the problems the Jewish people were experiencing at the hands of the Nazis. Uncle's work kept him late at his office, and, when he wasn't at work, he had other meetings to attend, so Aunt Rosa and I often had time alone in which to discuss such matters. We'd sit in the apartment, crocheting or knitting, and she would make occasional remarks like, "Those poor people!" "It's such a shame!" "I don't know why God doesn't stop this."

Eventually, I came to realize to the fact that, when she made such comments, she was referring to the plight of the Jews and that terrible things were happening to them; but I wasn't quite sure what these things were. Aunt Rosa warned me not to say anything about the subject to anybody except her. And, even then, she cautioned, I was only to discuss it when we were alone. Aunt Rosa had had many Jewish friends over the years because of her advertising work. She also had several contacts who kept her very well-informed about what Hitler was really doing to the Jews, not only in Munich, but throughout Germany. She told me that she was trying to help as many Jews as she could to get out of Germany. "Before Hitler kills them all," she concluded.

I had a hard time understanding what she was saying. "You mean, they have to *die?*"

She explained that Hitler and the Nazis hated the Jews and wanted to get rid of them. Hitler's men weren't just making them leave the country anymore; indeed, they were actually killing them! "It is already very bad for them, Agneška. Very bad. And it is going to get even worse. I must do all I can to help. I will tell you more later."

Aunt Rosa was especially concerned about me saying things at school concerning her feelings about the Jews. Many of the children, including my classmates, were members of the *Hitler Jugend* (Hitler Youth) – or "those damn brats," as Aunt Rosa always referred to them. In any case, they saw it as part of their duty to report any suspicious-sounding talk to the authorities. What was more, the school faculty and those students, who were part of the Hitler Youth, were constantly pressuring other students, including me, to become members.

Once, some Nazis came through our apartment building, distributing cloth squares with swastikas on them. They ordered us to display them in our apartments – by sewing them onto a sofa pillow, for example. The swastikas were black on a white background; and, since Aunt Rosa couldn't refuse the cloth without making trouble for my uncle and herself, she did sew it onto a pillow as instructed. Before she did so, however, she dyed the cloth black, making the swastika practically invisible. I realized later that she did this purely for her own purposes. Indeed, her hatred of that Nazi symbol was so intense that, many times during the war, she would take out her anger by picking up the pillow and spitting on the swastika.

★ ★ ★

One night in October, I asked if she wanted me to help her with whatever it was she was doing for the Jews.

"Not yet, Agneška," she answered. "I still want you to learn to speak Italian. My friend, the Baron Mader, who is a Jew, has an apartment in Rome. His daughter, Rosa, is also thirteen, the same as you. You only have to stay in Italy for four months. Baron Mader's daughter is learning English and you will learn Italian. She has two teachers to help you. But you will leave there in November, come back here for Christmas, and then return to Italy in January 1942. Then you'll be home to Munich at the end of February. You will have a lot of fun with Rosa. You will help her learn English and she will help you with Italian."

This trip of mine was only the latest episode in Aunt Rosa's continuing love affair with Italy. She was hungry for the sun and nowhere more so than in Italy. Whenever she had the opportunity, even for only a weekend, she would go to Venice, Rome, or anywhere along the northern Mediterranean. And she often had such chances, because many of her friends from the advertising business were well-to-do and Uncle's architectural practice was so busy that he didn't mind her being gone.

Even in Germany during the winter, Aunt Rosa's craving for the sun was quite apparent. Whenever there was a bright, cloudless day, she would put a lawn chair out in the *snow* and cover herself with blankets, just to feel the rays of the sun on her face.

In any case, my uncle gave his approval on my Italian trip; but he did not often accept the things my aunt planned. I frequently overheard them in the apartment talking not only about me, but about my aunt's activities in general. "Why are you doing all this?" he'd ask her, referring, I think, to the various trips and the language training I was receiving. And I could tell from the tone of his voice that he asked less out of anger, than out of concern about what would happen to Aunt Rosa and me if we were caught doing something suspicious. He seemed to know that my aunt was up to something, but she steadfastly refused to tell him about her other "work."

Part of that work included getting me over the Alps to learn Italian – which I did, as planned, in November of 1942. I had met Baron von Mader and his daughter, Rosa several times since I had arrived in Munich; so we all knew and liked each other. The

Baron's grandfather had been a successful business-man who'd established the family fortune. The current Baron von Mader, Rosa's father, continued to be involved in the family business and he, therefore, traveled a great deal.

When we were in Italy, we always stayed in one of the Baron's villas or the private homes of his friends. The only times we stayed in hotels were when one of the Baron's friends owned said establishment. I certainly had a wonderful time in Italy, and, again, I think the biggest reason for this was because I was with Rosa Mader, a girl friend my own age. Most of the time we only had one teacher and there were very few other grownups around. So we felt we could act much "older" and more independent. We had a car and a chauffeur at our disposal, so our teacher was often able to take Rosa and me on short trips into the coun-tryside around where we were staying. We visited Rome, Milan, Verona, and especially Venice. I'm sure the scenery was beautiful, but Rosa and I, being so young, were much more focused upon having fun. We played games, talked and joked with each other. In Venice, we rode the gondolas through the many canals; but my Italian was still pretty rough, so I referred to them as "the little ships."

My stay in Italy was a refreshing change from home, where Aunt Rosa kept a very tight rein on all of my activities. As I have mentioned, she didn't believe in my being with other kids. Many times, I stood on the balcony of our apartment and watched longingly as the neighbor's children played below. But I was not able to go down and join them because my aunt for-bade it. It seemed somewhat cruel at the time; but, in light of my subsequent secret work during the war, I understood better why Aunt Rosa trained me the way she did.

CHAPTER FIVE

MYSTERIOUS TRANSLATIONS

Before I knew it, the first part of my stay in Italy was over and I returned to Munich for Christmas of 1941. My sister Rosa was very happy when I came home, but very sad when I again had to leave for Italy after the holidays. While I was there, however, my sister Rosa attended a private school which was run by Catholic nuns. There they taught her to knit, crochet, and embroider; and, by the time I returned for good from Italy in February 1942, she had knitted me a scarf, a cap, and a pair of gloves!

★ ★ ★

At Easter we spent two weeks at the Villa Waldeck, while my uncle stayed behind in the city working on completing an eleven-story building in Munich for his architectural firm, Karl Steor. It was the highest office building in the city at the time. Its elevator was of the older variety and, therefore, did not stop at individual floors. Thus, the passengers had to step on and off as the car moved slowly between floors. Some people were scared to take this

View of Bavarian Mountains with St. Margarethen (right), Hochsalwand (center), and Wendelstein Mountain (left).

elevator because of its constant movement and the open car. But climbing eleven flights of stairs wasn't much better.

The spring of 1942 was extraordinarily beautiful. The grass in the mountain meadows grew lush and green. The alpen rose, enzian, and edelweiss were in bloom, creating splashes of dark pink, blue, and white against the green of the meadows and forests.

One day, my sister Rosa and I took the cog-rail train up Wendelstein mountain, just behind the villa. Wendelstein stands 1,840 meters (or 6,036 feet) high. On the very top of the peak was an observatory for studying the sun. At that time, it was Europe's largest and highest observatory. It also had radio antennas, UKW cables, and other technical equipment which allowed radio communication for hundreds of miles

79

in all directions. For many years, the observatory had also been used by the German military and other Nazis as a communications post. It became an especially important site, as German forces spread out across Europe and into Russia. It allowed the authorities to stay in touch with these far-flung units, and this was, naturally, extremely important to the war effort.

Several hundred feet below the observatory was a hotel, which was the end of the line for the cog-rail train. This hotel was a popular place, not only for people staying there, but for tourists and visitors who made day trips up to Wendelstein. For about an hour and a half, the train my sister Rosa and I rode chugged through many tunnels and climbed steep slopes of nearly 45 degrees pitch before reaching the hotel.

We had chosen a beautiful day to go up to Wendelstein. The sky was a deep, cloudless blue and the mountains looked purple. Some of their peaks still wore the white crowns of winter's snow, and these contrasted stunningly with the greens of the valleys below and the golden-silver sunlight which reflected off the streams and rivers far beneath us.

As we got off the cog railway at the hotel, we could see the Austrian, Italian, and Swiss Alps, since all three of these countries were within that glorious, sun-filled view. The wooden walkway from the hotel to the observatory was quite literally nailed to the side of the mountain. So, unless visitors didn't mind looking down a sheer drop of thousands of feet, they stayed close to the wall. The walkway was quite narrow, with barely enough room for two people to get past each other on it. Because of the steepness of the slope, the walkway had many switchbacks, so I often

Wooden walkway that led from hotel to observatory. Looking down on clouds with peaks of other mountains showing through.

wondered whether I was going forward or backtracking when I was on it. But one always traveled upward upon it, and, after about 30 minutes, my sister and I finally reached the top.

From the observatory grounds, the sight was breathtaking. In the valley far below to the south was the little town of Bayrischzell, and beyond, to the south-southeast, we could look over into Italy. To the east we could look back toward St. Margarethen and the valley of the River Inn. On nearby mountains we could make out the gemsen or mountain goats. They looked, from that distance, like small dots, moving singly and in groups, seemingly straight up the vertical slopes.

Surprisingly, going back down the mountain was much harder than climbing up – not only on the legs, but because one simply couldn't help looking down. My sister Rosa got a bit dizzy on this, her first trip. Consequently, she really stuck close to the mountain side of the walkway. When we arrived at the hotel, she slumped to the ground. This was, she claimed, partly out of exhaustion and partly out of gratitude for finally being on solid ground once more and no longer suspended thousands of feet in the air on a couple of wooden planks.

The hotel staff didn't mind that people who were day tripping up the mountain brought their own food with them. So we'd packed some bread, cheese, and sausage in our rucksacks and we ate them at the hotel before reboarding the cog-rail train to go down the mountain to Villa Waldeck. By 5:00 p.m. we were walking back to the villa after a beautiful day on the mountain.

Wendelstein with observatory. Hotel and cog-rail station below.

As we drew near the villa, we saw a very unusual sight: a car parked inside the gate. We thought that my uncle might have left it there. But he very seldom took the company car and its driver up to the villa. The mystery grew deeper as we walked into the house and spotted six strangers in the living room; yet there was no sign of my uncle. As soon as we came in the door, Aunt Rosa told the two teachers, "Take Rosa upstairs. Help her change clothes and get washed up. Agnes, I want to talk to you."

I knew in that instant that something was definitely up!

While my sister and the teachers marched up the stairs to the second floor, Aunt Rosa took me into the living room. "Agnes," she said, "these three couples are our friends and they will be staying for a couple of weeks. Then they will be leaving for England. I want you to write a letter in English for them in the morning. Say nothing to your sisters or your teachers about this. I will make whatever explanations are necessary."

The mystery only grew deeper. As I went to bed that night, I wondered what these people could possibly be doing at the villa. And why was my aunt involved with them? It occurred to me that perhaps they were related to Professor Sauter, the English-woman next door. And what would they ask me to write for them in the morning? As I fell asleep, these questions buzzed around my head like a swarm of gnats.

After breakfast the following day, two of our six visitors dictated a two-page letter to me in German, which I, in turn, wrote down in German, since I could not yet do "simultaneous translation." I took this

German version of the letter up to my room where I translated it into English. This was very hard work, and it didn't help that Aunt Rosa would frequently come up and interrupt me only to ask, "How is it going?"

She was obviously very concerned, not only about getting the translation done, but about whether I was capable of it. I think this was because this was the first time I had really put my language training to use in her "work." In any case, it seemed that I would *never* get those pages done.

But, when, at last, I did, I turned the finished English translation over to my aunt. I have no idea what she did with it, but she seemed very proud of me for completing the task. It was not easy to tell when Aunt Rosa was pleased or proud of me, because she didn't show her feelings very much. And she was especially careful not to become too demonstrative with me, because she believed that would get in the way of the work for which she was preparing me.

This time, however, she put her hand on my shoulder and gave it a squeeze. Since Aunt Rosa had tremendous strength in her arms and hands from years of cutting wood for the villa, the painful pressure of her grasp nearly made my knees buckle under me. Nevertheless, I knew that this was her way of telling me how pleased she was with the work I had done on the mysterious translation.

Within two weeks, she received a reply to my letter which contained information about what these six people had to do to reach England and precisely how they had to do it. On the way back to Munich, Aunt Rosa made both my sister and I promise not to say a word to my uncle about the people staying in the Villa. What she didn't say was that he wouldn't understand what his wife was doing helping Jews escape from Nazi Germany.

★ ★ ★

From April to June of 1942, I followed a regular schedule of activities. I continued working on all of the languages I had learned. And I continued my studies in arithmetic and geography, both of which I loved. I also took ballet and tumbling lessons to keep me fit and strong.

It was about this time that I made friends with a couple of German girls from school. Both of them were members of the Hitler Youth, and they wanted to get me to join as well. They even gave me a Hitler-Youth jacket to wear home one day. I really wanted to be liked by these new friends, so I felt rather proud about wearing the jacket home. No sooner had I gotten in the door, however, than Aunt Rosa was grilling me about it.

"Where did you get that jacket? Who gave it to you? Why are you wearing it?" The questions came at me so fast that I scarcely had time to answer.

She took the jacket from me and held it by her fingertips at arm's length, as if it were infested with some sort of deadly vermin. "I'd throw this rag into the stove and burn it," she growled, "except that it would cause too many problems!"

Once her anger had subsided, she talked to me about the Hitler Youth and why I couldn't wear the jacket ever again. "I know you want to have friends, Agneška. But girls who wear such things are not your friends. They are the enemies of the people we are helping. And they would think nothing of getting you in trouble, if it would make them popular with the Hitler Youth leaders. The work we are doing together is dangerous. Being friends with these girls will make it even more so. You could say something to them that would put us all in danger, without even realizing what you had said. Under no circumstances should you bring them to the house." she concluded sternly.

Even though I knew that Aunt Rosa was right, I ached inside at these orders from her because I so wanted to have friends my own age – especially after having been allowed to do so during my stays in Paris and Italy. So we kept the jacket, rather than burning it. But my aunt hid it away and I never again wore it. Nor did I join the Hitler Youth. And, just as Aunt Rosa had predicted, those girls didn't stay my friends for very long, not once they realized I wasn't going to join their group.

★   ★   ★

When summer vacation finally arrived in July, we left Munich to spend it at the villa. We arrived to find that eight new Jewish friends were already waiting for us there, hidden away in my aunt's secret room in the cellar. They were going over the mountains to Switzerland at the end of July and I was to accompany them. My role would be to play what my aunt called "the goat": the child who would make them look like a family unit and, thereby, cause them to be less suspect to the authorities. I would also act as their translator, since I was now able to speak all of the languages used in Switzerland: German, English, and French.

Aunt Rosa said, "Agneška, the plans have changed at the last minute; so now there will be two cars driving to Bern, Switzerland. Your uncle will bring Mila with him here to the villa, so that your sister Rosa will have some company while you are gone. Rosa can also help Mila with the cooking and cleaning and still have fun."

The day before my uncle and sister Mila arrived, I left with the eight Jewish people. We set out early in the morning and I remember little of the trip to Bern, Switzerland, except being awakened occasionally from my light sleep in the back seat of the car by the twisting and turning of the mountain roads.

Once in Bern, I stayed in a hotel with one of the Jewish couples for two weeks. I was later told that they needed to have a child, so that they could register to stay in Switzerland. Those seemed the longest two weeks of my life up to that point! There were no children in the hotel, and, even if there had been, I wouldn't have been able to play with them, since my adult companions and I rarely left our room. According to my aunt, the people whose "daughter" I was playing were very well-known Jews. Thus, they did their utmost to keep a low profile in Bern. It later occurred to me that perhaps they were waiting to make their way on to England or the United States; but I never knew for sure.

In any case, for a teenage girl, the daily boredom of this two-week hotel-room confinement was appalling. All I could do was read, draw, look out the window, listen to music on the radio, eat, and sleep. There were times when I felt like bursting out the door and running down the hotel hallways – just for the sake of having something different to do!

Finally, however, the two weeks came to an end and the couple disappeared. One morning they left the room after breakfast and told me to remain there. They instructed me to open the door of the room only when I heard a special pattern of three knocks. A short while later, I heard this code of knocks at the door, and, when I opened it, the woman standing on the threshold greeted me by name and introduced herself as my new English teacher. She then took me to another hotel at the opposite end of Bern. Clearly, whoever was organizing the operation didn't want to risk my being seen with someone other than the Jewish couple with whom I had come into the country. Had this happened, it would have been far too obvious that I had simply been playing the part of "the goat."

★ ★ ★

I stayed with my new English teacher for a couple of months in Bern. I attended school three days a week. It was a very full day, with classes from eight in the morning until five in the evening. I brought my own lunch and I had plenty of time to play outside during the noon hour. This school assigned lots of homework, but I still had time to take tumbling lessons every day. I also got to skip rope and roller-skate with kids my own age. What a wonderful contrast it was to the two weeks I'd spent cooped up in that first hotel room!

★ ★ ★

In October of 1942, I returned to Munich. I was delighted to see my aunt and uncle again, when they picked me up at the train station! By the time we got to the apartment, my sister Rosa was home from school.

My English teacher had taken some pictures of me in Bern and she gave them to me to take back to Germany. The photos showed me at the school and playing with the other kids. As my uncle listened to me narrate these pictures for him and my aunt and sister, he smiled broadly. It was only then that I realized I was not speaking German! Indeed, I was explaining the photos in a combination of English, German, and French, just as I'd had to do in Bern. I was so overjoyed to be home that I had forgotten I was no longer in Switzerland!

My uncle was very happy to see how well I was doing with French and English, because he believed that being able to speak a second language – let alone a *third* and a *fourth* – was the mark of an educated person.

When I realized what I was doing while narrating the photos, I said in German with a laugh, "I must still think I'm in Bern!"

My uncle reached out and hugged me. It was the first hug he'd ever given me, and it meant so much to me because I finally knew that he liked me.

I would have appreciated a hug from my aunt as well, but that simply wasn't her style. Instead, she just smiled and said, "Agneška, you are doing really well. Very soon you will again have the opportunity to use all of your languages."

CHAPTER SIX

CODE NAME: 3-6-9 KID

"Agneška, it is time for you to get to work. For the past two and a half years you have learned several languages and traveled throughout Europe. These things you will now put to use," Aunt Rosa declared in her usual blunt manner.

I had been wondering for some months, as the war had raged across Europe and beyond, whether she had something in mind for me, something that would involve me in more of her mysterious activities. Nevertheless, my aunt made it clear that I should continue in school. She wanted me to keep up with my normal activities and schooling like any other 14 year old. That is to say, she wanted my life to be as "normal" as it could be in a country at war with the rest of the world.

By "work" my aunt was indeed referring to her secret activities, the work I had caught glimpses of as strangers came and went, speaking only in whispers or behind closed doors. At 14, I certainly felt old enough to help my aunt, but I was so short and petite that people often thought I was only ten or eleven. This bothered me because I didn't want to be thought of as a child, when, in fact, I was already a young woman. But Aunt Rosa told me that my size and child-like appearance would be great advantages in the work she had in mind for me. She explained that a little girl would not attract attention in public and the authorities would hardly expect someone so young to be doing whatever it was she had planned for me. In an emergency, I could easily lose myself, like a tiny mouse, among a crowd or on a busy street.

"I am glad you have done so well in your studies and have such a quick mind," my aunt continued. "I will need your help because things are getting very bad and we must do what we can to help."

In spite of the compliment, I wasn't quite sure what Aunt Rosa meant regarding "things getting bad." I was sure, however, that some of it had to do with the Jews. I had noticed that the situation for them in Munich was becoming worse. I'd seen them wearing the Star of David on their clothes since my arrival; but now I noticed a change in their looks and appearances. Their faces were downcast, their coat collars were pulled up to masking heights, and they invariably wore looks of worry or fear. But, perhaps most ominously, we couldn't help noticing an increase in trains and other traffic around the camp at Dachau, just north of Munich.

I remembered what Aunt Rosa had told me about the Nazis and their feelings toward the Jews, and it made me both sad and angry. And I thought of my friend Martha back in Slovakia and wondered if she too was wearing the Star of David or whether she

Cog-rail train in foothills of St. Margarethen, Villa Waldeck (center) with church to left and English professor's home on the right.

would soon be riding one of the trains.

These thoughts came back to me one rainy day in September of 1942, when Aunt Rosa and I took the train from Munich out to the Villa Waldeck. We knew, however, that we were not alone. A short distance behind, four men and two women were following us. We knew only that they were Jews from the Munich area and that our mission was to safely house them on this leg of their escape from Germany. As we walked from the train station and up the road toward the Villa Waldeck, they followed, strung out in pairs or singly. They were dressed neatly for traveling, most of them carrying nothing more than overnight bags.

Aunt Rosa and I had reached the house, and she remained in front by the gate and gave a pre-arranged signal to the Jews, which told them this was the place and that the way was clear. They were supposed to

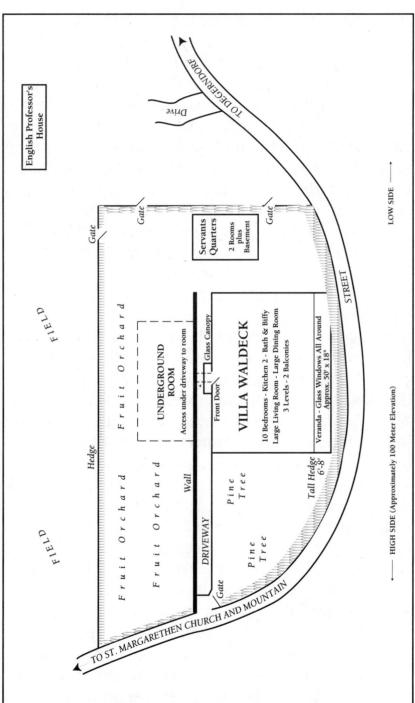

Map of Villa Waldeck and its grounds

walk past at a normal pace, receive the signal, and then return down the road. Then, looking carefully to make certain that no one was in the area, they would come around the rear of the villa and enter through the yard. Fortunately, the back and sides of the villa were surrounded by trees, so no one could see people entering through the back gate. And we were doubly lucky in that there were no neighbors to the front of us. In fact, the nearest home in that direction was a small farmhouse which was over a quarter of a mile up the road. With six people coming into the villa at once, we had to be careful not to attract attention. But, little by little, the task was accomplished and, by nightfall, we had all of them safely hidden in the basement.

Once in the house, I led them down the stairs and into a hallway to the right, which ran the length of the cellar. We walked past the storage rooms, which held the two kinds of coal used to heat the villa. This hallway appeared to end in a brick wall, which formed the foundation of the villa. However, some of these foundation bricks were mounted on a heavy wooden door – creating the appearance of a seamless wall. This door, which seemed to me as heavy as that of a bank vault, opened into a 10-foot-by-14-foot room containing eight cots, some small tables and chairs, and a wash basin. The room extended beyond the villa, running underneath both the driveway and the apple- and pear-tree-filled yard.

Ventilation to this chamber was supplied by a small pipe, which stuck up into the lawn and was hidden by brush and other vegetation. Even with ventilation, the air became stale when the room was full. And, if a guest was sick or injured, this could become a problem. Thus, for such emergencies, we kept oxygen tanks and masks in the room to help our ailing guests breathe.

Bathroom facilities were no different from the rest of the villa, which had no running water. So, everyone used chamber pots.

Late at night, when everybody upstairs was asleep, our "guests" could leave the room and walk around in the basement to get some exercise. But, during the day, my aunt checked in on them regularly; and their stays with us usually lasted three to four days – but sometimes as long as a week.

★ ★ ★

The weather had turned rainy several days before the arrival of our six guests, and the road in front of the villa had become badly rutted and full of potholes. It was a fairly steep mountain road and not in good condition in the first place. So, within a day of our secret visitors' arrival, the stretch of it that ran just in front of the villa was filled with 40 to 50 French prisoners-of-war who were being forced to repair it. They were surrounded by heavily-armed German guards and, given that my aunt and I had half a dozen Jewish refugees hiding no more than 50 yards away from them, I saw it as a very dangerous situation. But Aunt Rosa took a different view. Where I saw only danger, she also saw opportunity.

The Germans routinely used prisoners of war in civilian projects like road repair. At this time most of the POWs in our area were French, although the occasional British or American turned up as well. This particular work detail arrived each day at 9:00 a.m. They were standing in the back of large, army trucks which rolled noisily up the road, gears shifting and engines roaring. They came from the prisoner-of-war (POW) camps in Rosenheim and Bad Aibling, which were about 20 kilometers away. The men jumping down from the trucks in front of the villa looked similar to prisoners we had seen on other work details in the Munich area. Most still wore the uniforms they had been captured in, now two or three years old. And the holes and tears in their clothes, combined with their dirty, unshaven faces and the rainy weather, added to an overall sense of depression and melancholy. It pained me terribly to see the guards with their guns every day, to say nothing of the sad, sullen faces of the prisoners right in front of our beautiful villa.

The six or seven guards assigned to this work detail were very strict. None of the prisoners were allowed to talk while they were working. Occasionally, I would see them share a cigarette. But even that was done with a bare minimum of interaction and without breaking the rhythm of their work. As soon as all the prisoners were out of the trucks, the guards lined them up and took a head count to make sure they had the same number of prisoners they'd left the camp with. Then the tools were quickly distributed and the men set to work.

Throughout the morning, they used picks and shovels to fill in holes, remove rocks, and smooth the surface of the road. At lunch time they were given a 20-minute break, during which a prisoner carried a box of sandwiches up and down the rows of men. Each one took a sandwich and sat eating silently. When lunch was done, they resumed work until 4:00

p.m. Then they were lined up once more for a head count, the tools were gathered by the guards, and all of them boarded the trucks for the return to the prison camp.

As I said, I viewed the presence of the work detail with trepidation. How on earth were we going to get the six Jews out of the cellar, with armed soldiers in front of the house all day? But Aunt Rosa was determined to make the best of a bad situation. Not only would we get our secret guests out safely, she maintained, but we were going to snatch a French prisoner or two right out from under the noses of those guards! What was more, she was counting on me and my ability to speak French to help her carry out this plan.

No language exam I had taken was ever like this! At first I didn't know whether I was more afraid of the prisoners or the guards. The prisoners, after all, were prisoners; and, with their gaunt faces and shabby clothes, it was hard not to think of them as criminals. But the guards were even more terrifying, with their rifles always at the ready and the long bayonets in their scabbards hanging from their belts. I was sure that, if they even suspected what I was doing, they would shoot me on the spot.

But Aunt Rosa had already planned everything out carefully. The first day we watched closely from the house. Then, around 10 or 11 a.m., my aunt, my sister Rosa, and I walked out through the gate and approached the work party. Aunt Rosa talked to one of the German guards. And my sister, who knew nothing about what my aunt and I were up to, played innocently at the feet of another guard. All of this activity was meant to divert attention from me. My first task was to get between the guards and the prisoners, without being noticed. My size and youthful appearance would make it look like I was doing as my younger sister was – simply playing. But that day, my real goal was to communicate with the prisoners.

Aunt Rosa had told me what questions to ask them. I was to inquire quickly in French, "What Company?" (meaning what army unit did they belong to?) Then, without waiting for an answer, I was to ask, "How many in Camp? X3" The X3 was a code number which identified me so that the prisoners knew it was safe to talk to me.

It should have been easy. I just had to ask two simple questions. Yet, as I played around by the road, there was always a guard no farther than ten to fifteen feet from me, his eyes constantly moving up and down the column of prisoners and his rifle poised for the least sign of trouble. I felt as if those guards' eyes were looking right through me, that they could see inside my mind and recognize my intentions. Nonetheless, I kept concentrating on my mission. I picked up a stick and began to draw in the dirt at the side of the road. This led me near some of the prisoners, and I began to ask my questions in French. I had to do it very quietly, literally under my breath, and without moving my lips much. Yet my voice had to be loud enough for the prisoners to hear. What was more, I couldn't make eye contact with them or even look in their direction as I spoke. And I had to concentrate on my listening, because, if any of them dared to reply, it would be hardly louder than the rustling of the leaves on the nearby apple trees.

I had moved passed several prisoners, asking my questions, and I'd gotten no response. I did notice, however, that all of their eyes were now on me. They weren't really staring, but each would glance at me regularly, as they continued working. Only years later did I stop to think what a shock it must have been for them, having been prisoners of war for over three years, to suddenly hear this 13-year-old girl whispering a code to them in French which indicated that I was a secret agent who could help them escape. No wonder they were slow to respond!

Some of them probably thought it was some sort of trick. But, within seconds of my first whispered message, the entire work crew seemed to know that something out of the ordinary was going on; and I could tell that they were just holding their breaths, waiting to see what would happen next. Would some contact really be made for an escape? Or was I simply part of a Nazis trap? Would they ever be free again? Or were they fated to spend the rest of their lives digging with shovels and picks on muddy roads deep inside Germany?

At last, on my fourth or fifth try, I got an answer. I quickly memorized it, as well as the face of the French soldier who uttered it. Then I returned to slowly skipping about and picking up rocks, as I worked my way back to my sister and Aunt Rosa. My sister and I went back to the villa, while my aunt stayed out by the fence to make sure we were safely inside. My part for the day was over. But the tension and pressure was so intense that I felt as if I had been out on that road for hours. Yet Aunt Rosa told me later that only five or ten minutes had passed before I returned to her.

After my sister had gone upstairs and Aunt Rosa had come back in, I told her the French prisoner's reply. Her face showed no emotion, but her eyes took on that sparkle which indicated that she was pleased. I was glad to see this, because I had no idea what the response from the French prisoner meant. Aunt Rosa had not told me what the codes stood for.

"And you will not know tomorrow either," she said sternly, maintaining an air of secrecy. It was clear, however, that the first part of Aunt Rosa's plan had been accomplished: contact with the French soldiers had been made.

The next day, the prisoners were out working again, and I knew that my aunt was about to implement the next part of her plan. This time Aunt Rosa, my sister and I went out to the road with beer and cigarettes for the guards. These unexpected treats so completely distracted them, that I was able to get more information from the prisoner who'd spoken to me, without the guards even realizing I was doing so. I would later learn that the soldier with whom I was communicating was an officer. And my task now was to speak the following words to him in French: "X3 is ready for six or seven."

He replied with a code of his own. "Four is ready," he whispered.

As on the day before, I had no idea what these codes meant, since my job was simply to act as a messenger. I found out later that my codes referred to locations for further information about the escape network that would help him flee from Germany. But, obviously, he had to escape from the work detail first.

★ ★ ★

On the third day, the prisoners were back once more, and so were we, this time around mid-afternoon. After the beer and cigarettes of the day before, my aunt was quite popular with the guards and they were chatting with her at some length. The party had completed their work in front of the villa and had moved about 500 feet up the road from our front gate.

I was given another code to relay to the French officer. This time, however, my aunt had told me what the code meant. It instructed the officer to slip away from the work detail while the guards were distracted. He was to come around to the back of the villa, where the fence and the trees would screen him from sight. It was my job to quietly return to the villa, while my aunt and sister continued to talk with the guards. From there, I would meet the French officer and take him to our underground room.

Everything worked exactly as Aunt Rosa planned. I met the French officer at the back gate and led him into the house and down to the underground room. Then I opened the door and saw our six Jewish refugees look up at me. Now there would be seven, and the room would be a little crowded. But seven was, after all, a lucky number. And, indeed, the seventh of our guests was lucky. In fact, he was not missed until the guards conducted their head count just before returning to camp; so they couldn't be certain exactly when he'd escaped.

My part of the operation had ended when I'd put him in the underground room; but we knew that, once his absence was discovered, there would be a house-to-house search of the area. That evening, my sister and I were reading in the living room. Of course, my sister knew nothing about what had gone on that day; and, in truth, even I had no idea what had become of our seven guests since I had left them that morning. So when the guards came to search the villa, they asked us if anyone else was in the house, and we said, "no." As it turned out, that was the absolute truth. They searched every room from top to bottom, but did not discover our secret chamber. Even if they had, however, they would have found it empty. Indeed, the "lucky seven" had long since been moved on to the next stop on their way out of Germany.

After the guards left and my sister was out of the room, my aunt took my hand and looked at me, her eyes again sparkling, yet steady. "Agneška," she said, "we have done really well! Today, we saved seven lives."

★ ★ ★

The day after our secret guests left the villa, we returned to Munich. It was a beautiful, sunny September morning, with just a hint of autumn in the air, and we arrived to find lots of activity in the city. The reason for the activity was soon clear. Hitler was in town and, that afternoon, he would be part of a parade. My aunt made no bones about her hatred of him, so it was a foregone conclusion that she would not come with my uncle and me to the parade. But, unfortunately, my uncle's situation was different. He had no choice but to put on a front, because he was one of the top architects in Munich. To get work he had to play along with the Nazis, since they controlled the construction of all the big buildings. He was never, himself, a Nazi; yet many of his best friends were. I think he was uncomfortable with this state of affairs, but it was lucky for Aunt Rosa and I that Uncle had the "friends" he had. Many times he had to call on them for favors to keep my aunt out of prison or worse predicaments, because she occasionally revealed her true feelings about the Nazis. In return for their help with Aunt Rosa, my uncle would design their houses and help them find building materials, which were very scarce during the war.

So that afternoon, as the sun gave way to a light overcast, my aunt stayed home and only my uncle and I walked down to the parade route. Nazi flags and banners hung from the buildings and lamp posts all up and down Hindenburger Strasse. There were thousands of people standing on the sidewalks and curbs along the parade route. Many wore Nazi arm bands, which were strips of red cloth, about four inches wide, with a white circle containing a black swastika.

Long ranks of German soldiers marched by us with stiff-legged goose-steps. Their faces were rigid and they seemed to be staring at some faraway point. I remember especially the clomp, clomp, clomp of their brightly polished black boots in perfect time on the pavement. Their neat uniforms, their glistening rifles, and the soft clank of their equipment against their belts, as they marched, added to the powerful effect of so many men on the move. Thus, it was hard for me to make a connection between these sharply turned-out men and the sullen guards standing in the drizzle out at the Villa Waldeck. But the thought occurred to me that, for all I knew, those very guards could have been part of the columns marching in front of us at that moment.

Then the noise from the tanks and armored cars was upon us like a tidal wave. Shortly thereafter, the vehicles themselves appeared. We began to see movement and hear loud shouts from the crowds up the street.

Hitler was coming. The first glimpse I caught of him was just of his head and shoulders, because he was far away and, given how short I was, I could only see up at an angle. Then my uncle helped me to get a better view, and I saw that Hitler was standing in the back of a huge open automobile. The movement and shouts were coming from people on the sidewalk, giving the Nazi salute and shouting, *"Heil! Seig Heil!"* as Hitler's car drove by. We saw several people who did not give the Nazi salute as he rode past. Either they forgot to or they simply chose not to do so. In any case, they were quickly yelled at by others in the crowd who demanded that everyone salute the Fuhrer. My uncle and I stood about 20 feet from Hitler as his car slowly rolled past. We too saluted him, our arms held straight out and slightly raised in front of us, and we shouted, *"Heil!"* Then Hitler turned toward the part of the crowd where my uncle and I stood and gave us all the Nazi salute in return. During the entire parade Uncle did not have much to say. And, when we returned to the apartment, Aunt Rosa greeted us sharply with, "You both wasted a beautiful afternoon!"

★ ★ ★

We spent the Christmas season of 1942 at the villa. For me that meant a time away from undercover activities and a break from schoolwork. Ironically, though, I actually seemed to get injured more when I was not working with my aunt. That Christmas was just such a time. We did a lot of skiing on Wendelstein mountain. We would start at the Wendelstein Hotel, which practically hangs on the side of the mountain. From there, it was a beautiful five-mile downhill run back toward St. Margarethen. After only one week's practice, I could ski down the mountain in about 50 minutes, which meant I could easily make two runs a day. But, on the eleventh day, my luck ran out. I hit a tree and was knocked unconscious.

Fortunately, we always skied with partners. However, on that particular day, it took my partner a while to realize that I was no longer behind him. He called for help, but nearly an hour passed before the rescue workers found me, still lying behind that tree. While I had no broken bones, a doctor visited me twice daily at the villa for several days, due to concern that I'd suffered a concussion or other head injury. I was lucky that, as it turned out, I hadn't sustained any damage to my head, because I would need all of my wits about me for the work that was soon to follow.

★ ★ ★

When we returned to Munich on January 4, 1943, I was still experiencing occasional dizzy spells. But my aunt was not deterred by my condition. Aunt Rosa had been very satisfied with my performance with the "Lucky Seven," and, throughout the autumn, I had continued to assist her by carrying messages and helping move refugees, escapees, and agents. Her trust in my abilities was growing, so she told me that I would now be given four days of special training. My task was to learn a system of codes so I could begin to operate more independently. Though Aunt Rosa would continue to watch over my work, she would, as I became more experienced, have less direct control and involvement with my missions.

I would be an important link in a chain of messengers and agents, who passed a variety of military and other information from spies and others to Allied intelligence officials. As a messenger, I rarely knew much about the content of the messages I carried. Everything was in code and my job was simply to carry the coded information to the next link in the chain of agents, who would eventually get it to the Allies.

Sometimes the codes were words and sometimes they were numbers or names – or a combination of these. Occasionally I would learn something about the content of a message. For example, for a while, a woman's name referred to an airplane. So, "Mary," for instance, stood for a Messerschmitt ME-109, a German fighter plane. Men's names referred to tanks or ships. But this was only for a while, because the codes were always changing. Even the code that identified me.

I received four or five different code names during my entire career as a spy. I was registered and my files were kept in Washington, D.C., so that I was official-ly a spy for the United States of America. But much of the information I was involved with actually went to U.S. personnel in London. I would also use my code number in face-to-face contacts with agents and spies in Germany.

In the beginning, Aunt Rosa gave me my code name and watched everything I did very carefully. For example, my first code name was 3-6-9. But my age and appearance often required that I provide some additional information. People as young as I was were very rare in espionage networks. And, unless they were informed otherwise, my contacts would be expecting an adult to meet them. So I know that, on more than one occasion, my contacts received not just my code name, 3-6-9, but 3-6-9 *KID*. Even so, I still saw surprise in many of their eyes when I first met them. Somehow, in spite of the add-on label "Kid," they just weren't expecting someone so childlike to be part of their secret network.

★ ★ ★

As the war went on and I became experienced and proved myself, my code names were given directly to me, rather than my aunt. Nevertheless, I found that it was still a good policy to add the "KID" onto my code name. I remember one later instance when I was using the radio to give someone my code name for a future contact, and I gave it as 3-6-9 KID, so they would be expecting a young person when we met.

The voice on the other end immediately came back through the static with, "Repeat something behind the nine."

I had to come back and repeat "K-I-D," even though it meant added danger because it forced me to transmit again. This party simply couldn't seem to comprehend that he should be expecting a kid as the contact in this case.

Aunt Rosa didn't like to call me a spy; but, of course, even when operating as a messenger, that was precisely what I was. Spies are not just people sneaking into locked offices in the dead of night to photograph secret documents. Much of the most dangerous work in espionage is the transmission of information. Carrying and relaying secret information is dangerous because it involves contact with other people and often in public, where one can be seen by the enemy.

Being a messenger also means being absolutely accurate. Not only could my life depend on going to the right place to meet the right person, but, if I did not remember the codes and information correctly, the work and deadly risks of many others, as well as myself, would have been wasted. What was more, if my transmission of the information was not one-hundred-percent accurate, it could cost the lives of those who would have to act on it. So I took my new responsibilities very seriously. I knew that my training in codes and messenger techniques meant a big increase in my responsibilities – as well as much more danger. I was still just 14 years old, and, when I realized the job I had to do, I was frightened half to death. Fortunately, I had Aunt Rosa to show me the way, so I felt that I was never truly alone in these efforts.

I never received any money from the U.S. govern-ment for my work. My reward, if I lived to collect it, was, that after the war, I could become an American citizen. For a poor Slovakian peasant girl, with few opportunities in my homeland, this was the greatest reward I could receive. Everyone knew that anything was possible in the United States. The hope of some-day living in America as a U.S. citizen kept my spirits up when the stress and danger of my work seemed overwhelming.

But that was still years in the future. For the time

being, I had to learn the rudiments of being a spy. To start with, that meant memorizing codes. And, during that cold January of 1943, even as word of the catastrophe of the German Army near Stalingrad was trickling back into Germany, I attended my first training meetings. Once again I realized that Aunt Rosa had been preparing me for this since the day I stepped off the train in Munich. Learning the four languages had given me not only the ability to translate and speak in different tongues, but it had strengthened and quickened my memory and mental reflexes. And the work of smuggling out refugees and POWs, which I had done under her direct supervision, had given me practice at making contact and operating in public without attracting attention.

For a time I would continue working under Aunt Rosa's supervision, until she was confident that I could operate reliably on my own. She would provide me with the information about who the contacts were and where and how I was to meet them. But, after that, it was up to me to rendezvous with the person who gave out the codes and receive and learn them on my own.

We were alerted to the need for a training meeting by a phone call. Initially, my aunt would take the calls, but later I was able to handle them by myself. Usually the "wrong number" technique was used to give the time and place for the meeting. The phone would ring at our apartment and the voice on the other end would sound puzzled, as if he or she had dialed the wrong number. This caller might say, "Is this 444?" And, when I replied, "no," he or she would say, "I'm sorry. I was looking for 446. I must have dialed incorrectly." Then the mysterious caller would hang up, but the numbers he or she mentioned were codes that meant, for example: meeting Wednesday, 6 p.m., at Frauen-Kirche, a Catholic Church.

No two training meetings were ever the same. Just as with the codes, the time, the location, and the "trainer" handing out the codes were always changing. The trainers were experienced agents, often ones who had been dropped by parachute into Germany by the Allies. They were usually Americans, but British intelligence officers and the occasional German resister gave us our information as well. Most of these sessions were conducted in English, yet it was clear that these people knew Germany better than I did.

We met in homes, churches, even hotels. Our main goal was not to draw attention to ourselves. So we'd act as though we'd come to these places for completely blameless purposes. For example, if we were meeting at a church, I would pretend I had come there to pray or visit the priest or pastor. The church officials were afraid to get directly involved with us because they were already bound by the strict laws and close scrutiny of the Nazis. But, since their churches were frequently left unlocked and people were visiting them at all times of the day and evening, they made excellent meeting places for training and for distributing new codes.

The length of our meetings varied, but they never exceeded an hour. By keeping our meetings short, we also avoided suspicion. No one would think, "I wonder why they are staying so long in church? They must have a lot of sins to pray for." It was just that kind of small question in someone's mind that would lead them to contact the authorities. Since the Nazis had come to power, they had been training and encouraging everyone to look for and report suspicious behavior by their neighbors or strangers. And, with the war on, German citizens saw it as their patriotic duty to the Fatherland to help identify spies and traitors.

Codes changed constantly. This was primarily for security reasons, but sometimes the content of the information changed as well. In any case, I found myself memorizing a new set of codes every two to six months. If an agent was caught, the codes would change immediately. A three- to four-month life span for a code set was typical. One frequent subject of the codes was troop movements and deployments. In the Munich area this usually referred to the Wehrmacht mountain divisions, as well as SS units.

Many of the details of these meetings are blurred in my memory. Partly because of the ever-changing faces, places, and times they entailed. But more so, I think this is because of the intense pressure I was under at the time. At these meetings we were making ourselves vulnerable to discovery or capture – even more so than when we were on actual missions. Thus, my inclination was to be constantly looking over my shoulder, listening for the faintest rustling of danger. The challenge, however, was to suppress such defense mechanisms. Rather than giving in to fear and nervousness, I had to use every ounce of my concentration to memorize new code sets, which usually consisted of 20 to 25 words or numbers and their respective meanings.

I often remember leaving the meetings feeling not only frustrated or scared, but physically dizzy, my head swimming with the information I had just received and working at top speed to get it embedded in my memory. Then, if I later received a coded message saying, "Didn't succeed," – meaning that the mission or operation I was working on had failed somewhere down the line – I remember sinking into deep depressions and despair.

Sometimes I could not memorize all of the codes correctly before I had to leave the meeting place. In such instances, I would write them on a piece of paper and carry it home in my mouth or tucked inside my bra. Then, as soon as I got home and finished committing the codes to memory, I burned the paper.

I remember an evening, when I was at one of these meetings, I was having trouble remembering three different codes I'd been given, so I wrote them down on a small slip of paper and folded it up into a tiny square. There were six of us underground workers at this meeting and I was the fourth to arrive at the church where it was being held. Unfortunately, I was the last one to leave, and, as I was exiting the church, I was stopped by a German policeman. Before he could spot the note I carried, I popped it into my mouth to hide it – poised to swallow it if he decided to search me.

He sternly pointed out that it was 9:00 p.m. and past the strictly enforced Nazi curfew time. Feigning tearfulness and tucking the note into one of my cheeks, so I could talk, I explained to him that I had been inside praying for my father, my mother, and my brothers who were in the war, and, therefore, I had forgotten how late it was getting.

I was terrified that he wouldn't believe me as he

continued to eye me suspiciously. I think it was even more frightening than the time a German soldier held a *knife* to my throat because I'd wandered into a building where I didn't belong!

Fortunately, my alleged "praying" must have paid off for me, because the policeman decided to let me go with just a warning. He patted my butt and said, "Hurry! Go home!"

But, because of this delay, I was about five minutes late getting home and my aunt didn't look like she was going to be as forgiving as the policeman had been. I explained what had happened, and I thought she was going to hit me! This would have been a very painful experience, indeed, since she was strong enough to split more logs than a man nearly half her age!

When she cooled down a bit, she explained that, with me doing such dangerous work, every minute that I was late getting home from such a meeting was like an *hour* to her. An hour spent agonizing over the possibility of my having been arrested or shot! I was only twelve at this time, but I understood, from that point forward, how perilous it was to linger behind after such meetings for any reason – to say nothing of the risks I took when I wrote down information which I had been strictly instructed to simply memorize.

I never had the chance to really talk with my fellow agents at our meetings. Firstly, we were very rushed to get our work done when we were together. But, most importantly, in order to maintain secrecy and protect the spy network, we knew each other only by code names or numbers. Since everyone I encountered in this regard was always much older than I was, they always called me the "kid" – just as I tagged on the end of my actual code name.

My fellow agents seemed to come from various walks of life. After some time I was able to discover that there were several doctors and professors involved. They usually arrived at our meetings dressed neatly in suits and ties and wearing fine-looking overcoats. Yet they were sometimes immediately followed into our gathering by Gypsies dressed in simple jackets and worn shoes. I could also tell that, while many of the agents were from the Munich area, others traveled from all over Germany to attend these meetings. They would never reveal precisely where they came from, but would sometimes speak of the distance they had traveled to reach our gathering. From this I was usually able to judge if they had come from as far away as Berlin or somewhere nearby there. I found these little details about the others reassuring. While I never really got to know any of them, I did feel as if I was part of something bigger and that it was not just Aunt Rosa and I doing this work alone.

None of us joked or otherwise showed much emotion at these meetings. Again, I'm sure everyone was as preoccupied as I was with the danger of the situation and memorizing the assigned codes. The tone was completely serious, and no one asked questions of anyone else. We simply got our codes and went on our respective ways. The one exception to this, however, was a professor who, after we had seen each other several times, took a moment to shake my hand and commend me for running such great risks at so young an age.

Of course, the professor was taking great risks as well, and, considering that he probably had a family and other responsibilities, who is to say which of us had the greater courage and daring? What was more, I was Slovakian, but he was German through and through. So, if he was caught at our undercover work, he would have been deemed a traitor to his country. Today, when Hitler has come to personify evil with a capital E, many think it would be an easy choice to fight a monster like him. But for people like that professor, it meant working against his own government and his own people.

Out of the 70 to 75 agents I met or worked with during the war, I only saw four after V-E Day. Of them, only one spoke to me, and, even then, all he said was, "Glad to see that you're alive." Thus, I learned, at an early age, that espionage is not a way to make friends or even to find comrades. On the contrary, it is a very lonely business.

Also, there were many with whom I had contact who did not survive. Often they were caught on their first missions. That's how important a part experience played in the success of an agent. So I was grateful knowing that my aunt had been preparing me for the past two years. Aunt Rosa also reminded me, however, that luck, ability, and quick-thinking had much to do with an agent's success or failure as well. "Some can do it and some can't," she said. And, although she didn't add it, I knew that she had a further thought which she held back. That being something along the lines of, "Unfortunately, there's only one way to find out whether you can or can't."

We all knew that capture meant certain death, usually after torture, but sometimes on the spot. I suppose that was one advantage of being so young; teenagers have a way of thinking of themselves as immortal. Danger, pain, fear: these things I knew. But I used to say that I was too stupid to worry about dying. I think now, however, that such an attitude is more a function of youth than a lack of intelligence.

★ ★ ★

When people think of a spy's equipment, tiny cameras, high-tech radios, and sophisticated weapons come to mind. But certainly not an *accordion*. Nevertheless, that was one of the first tools I used as a spy. After I finished my code training, Aunt Rosa purchased a 48-bass accordion for me (which I still own today). It was a large instrument and, I was so short, that I usually had to peek over the top of it in order to read the sheet music.

For most of the spring of 1943, as I turned 15, I took one-hour accordion lessons twice a week. I went to the music studio of a Mr. Pfeiffer, which was just a few blocks from our Munich apartment. Mr. Pfeiffer was unaware that, in addition to learning the music, I was also learning various signals to give out as I played. These included certain facial expressions or body movements when I reached a passage in the music that contained a code. I would convey these signals at certain places in the music to alert listeners to the notes which would follow. The agents attending the recitals were trained to recognize and remember the notes following my signal. Each note represented an assigned code word or number. For example, a G might be assigned the number five, which would indicate a five-letter word to follow. At first, I could not understand any of the codes; but, after several recitals, I began to catch on to some of them as I played.

Agnes with her accordion, the spring of 1943.

Even the titles of the well-known music I learned were part of the code system. *Schön Ist Die Liebe Im Hafen* (Beautiful is Love in Harbor) contained codes related to German naval operations. *Morgen Marchieren Wir* (Tomorrow We March Again) concerned troop movements. *Muss Ich Denn Zum Städtlein Hinaus* (I Have to Get Out of the City) and *Horch Was Kommt Von Draussen Rein* (Listen What is Coming in from the Outside) were cues that the information to follow was about Allied bombing missions.

In the spring of 1943, Mr. Pfeiffer and my aunt arranged for several of his students and me to begin a series of accordion recitals in schools, theaters, and restaurants throughout the Munich area. At each recital, Aunt Rosa had identified the codes which were worked into my pieces, and the agents who were to receive the messages were told to attend the recital. I saw many of the same people in the audiences at a number of these. And, while I knew that some of them were there to receive the codes I gave when I played my pieces, I never knew exactly which ones. At the same time, my aunt attended all of my recitals and was very proud of me.

In June 1943, I was invited to play at the Munich opera house with five other girls who were about my age. It was a Friday afternoon and roughly 60 or 70 people, mostly parents and children, were present. I was the last one to play. The title of my tune for that day was *Immer Lustig* (Always Happy), which indicated that I would smile to signal the agent or agents in the audience when a code was coming up. I had to be careful, however, not to smile until the designated point in my music, so that I didn't confuse the undercover listeners. On that particular day, the lyrics contained four messages concerning an Allied bombing attack which had occurred a few days earlier. These messages provided information about the bombing target, its location, its results, and whether another air attack was necessary. Not only was my music happy on that occasion, but so was I, because I found out that my messages helped to prevent a German attack from succeeding.

This communication method must have worked quite well because we performed about 20 such recitals over the following months. Nonetheless, I knew that my aunt was very nervous and scared – probably because these were such public events. Thus, as soon as the recitals were over, she quickly helped me pack up my accordion, then she rushed me back to our apartment.

★ ★ ★

In July and August of 1943, I really began to work on my own as an agent. Aunt Rosa felt that I had shown the ability and resources to receive my instructions and send my information directly, rather than having to work through her. But first, Aunt Rosa said that it was time for us to take a short trip together.

I asked why and to where, and she said, "There are things you must see. We are going to Dachau."

Aunt Rosa had explained earlier to me about the Nazis' hatred for the Jews. Many times we had seen Jews being herded, like so many animals, to and from trains or trucks. They would get off looking tired, run-down, and disoriented. The tracks of tears were still visible on the cheeks of some of them. Indeed, even the babies, children, and teenagers – many of whom were my age – appeared to have looks of confusion and fear permanently stamped on their faces.

They kept their eyes down or unfocused because to look at a guard, or a passerby, or even to glance upward meant a lash with a strap. Those Jews who were sick, crippled or otherwise had difficulty walking were whipped with a long leather strap an inch and a half thick. And, sometimes, an inch-wide horse whip was used on them. We could see those who were struck trying to choke back their screams and groans, because they knew that, if the guards heard them, they would get another lash across the back. If children were crying, their parents got the strap and a gruff, "Make them shut-up!" from the guards.

We also knew about the concentration camp in Dachau, a small town about 20 kilometers northwest of Munich, and that thousands of Jews had been sent there over the years. Now my aunt was making certain that I was aware of these things, so that I would understand the reasons why she and I were running the risks our underground work entailed.

Nevertheless, nothing my aunt had told me or that I had seen before prepared me for our trip to the concentration camp that day. Around noon we traveled from Munich to Dachau, taking the streetcar as far as we could. Then we walked another quarter mile or so through Dachau, to the point where we could see the perimeter of the camp.

We had a clear view of the two rows of barbed-wire fencing, which stood about 10-feet high. The square white guard towers, with their dark-colored pointed roofs, were placed along the fence, about every 150 yards or so. And I could see the silhouettes of the guards moving around inside them as they kept watch over the camp. We could not see the prisoners from the road; but covered trucks were busy coming and going from the camp.

As we drew closer, the air suddenly became thick and suffocating with an unbearable odor. I tried bending my head down to my chest in order to shield my nose from the stench. To say that the smell was sickening barely begins to describe it. Naturally, I asked Aunt Rosa what the cause of it was.

She pointed to the steady stream of smoke that was pouring from a tall chimney which stuck up amongst some trees in the camp. As I stood staring and trying to keep from throwing up, my aunt said, "That smoke is not from wood. There is not enough room for so many people to be buried, so they burn them. Their ashes don't take up any room; they just spread them over the fields. Agneška, they are no longer just imprisoning people in the camp. They are killing them – men, women, children, babies – the same ones you see coming in the trucks and the railroad cars."

Then she explained to me in exact, gruesome detail the inhuman things that were going on behind the fences at the Dachau camp. And she went on to say that even greater atrocities were happening at other camps far to the east in Poland. I have no idea how Aunt Rosa had acquired all of this information. But nothing I read subsequently about the operation of the camps contradicted anything she told me that day.

She said she knew she couldn't stop the killing and that her powerlessness over it made her angry and frustrated. And, as she spoke, there was great pain on her face, as if the very existence of that camp was like a dagger stuck in her side. One that she couldn't remove.

The tears were pouring down my cheeks faster than these words could leave my aunt's lips. I know my memory registered all that she said, yet I'm not sure my mind understood the enormous horror of what I was hearing, seeing, and smelling. Indeed, my reaction came from somewhere else, somewhere deep inside me. My tears were unlike any I'd cried before – or have since. They seemed not to come from my eyes, but from the pit of my stomach, with the uncontrollable force of a volcanic eruption. It was as if, on some basic, irrational level, my body understood what my mind couldn't or wouldn't and it was responding completely on its own, independently of my thoughts or ability to understand what was going on around me. Something at the very center of me, a 15-year-old girl, was somehow resonating with the unimaginable suffering and agony that was fouling the very air I breathed.

All of this must have happened in just seconds, because Aunt Rosa had barely stopped speaking when I looked up at her, my vision still blurred by tears, and met her steady gaze.

"Now that you have seen this, your job will get even more dangerous," she warned.

CHAPTER SEVEN

MISSIONS, MESSAGES AND A VISIT HOME

During the ride home from Dachau, neither my aunt nor I said much. What was there to say?

My throat still felt tight, and that horrible smell lingered in my nostrils even when we were back in Munich. Aunt Rosa's "shock treatment" had worked: I saw the work I was doing for her with a greater degree of seriousness than ever.

Prior to this time, I had been concerned about doing what she told me and not getting caught by the Nazis in carrying out her instructions. But now, I fully grasped the reason why I was living in danger. I understood why the risks I was taking were important, and I became more determined than ever to help as much as possible. If I was to do so, however, I realized I'd have to be even more careful not to give myself or my missions away.

When we got home, my uncle asked me where we had been, so I told him about our trip to Dachau. I assumed that my aunt had at least made mention of it to him. But I was wrong. I could tell by the tightening of her mouth as I answered him that I had unwittingly said too much.

As a result of my disclosure, Uncle became very upset with Aunt Rosa and they started to argue. He told her that I didn't need to see what was going on at the camp and that it was dangerous for her to have taken me there. Of course, he knew nothing of our undercover activities, so it was impossible for him to understand why it was important for me to visit such a place. Though it angered my aunt, I found Uncle's response quite touching, because it made me feel as if he was trying to protect me.

As always, however, I was much more concerned about what Aunt Rosa would have to say to me, than what my uncle had. I thought I might really be in for a tongue-lashing; yet later that evening, when she and I were alone, I found that she was stern but not angry.

"Your uncle doesn't think it's necessary for you to know about things like Dachau, but he's wrong. Now, having been there, I think you know why it's important. You needed to see that place. You're old enough and strong enough to take it in, however painful it may be. When you get into difficult situations, remember what you saw today; it will give you strength," Aunt Rosa said. "As for your uncle, be more careful about what you tell him. He doesn't know about everything that I am doing. And he certainly doesn't need to know about everything that goes on between you and me. Tell him nothing about any of our work or any other activity that is even remotely related to what we are doing, unless you first get permission from me. Are you clear about that?" she asked.

I assured her that I was.

In any case, my uncle had other matters on his mind besides keeping track of my comings and goings. For one thing, he was busy constructing an air-raid shelter in the basement of our five-story apartment building. German radio had made brief mention that British and American warplanes were flying over Berlin. The reports were full of propaganda, of course, but it was clear to everyone that those planes would soon be bombing Munich as well.

And only a month or so later, in the autumn of 1943, the Allied bombers did indeed begin attacking us, primarily at night. The air-raid sirens would go off between sunset and sunrise, so we had to be ready to make a run for the shelter any time after dark.

Each night, before I went to sleep, I placed my day clothes on the end of my bed, so that I could dress quickly, grab our suitcase, and rush down to the basement shelter which Uncle had just completed.

The first couple times I heard the sirens, they scared me so much that I almost passed out! I had never heard anything like it: that eerie tone that rose to a single high-pitched note, then seemed to wail on forever. Then it fell in pitch – only to rise again and wail some more. The sound alone would have been terrifying, but knowing that it would all too quickly be followed by falling bombs made me want to faint dead away!

Scrambling down the stairs in total darkness, we found our way to the shelter as much by sound as by sight. Once we reached the basement, there were a few dim lights to help us see. Then everyone in our apartment building crowded into the shelter. We sat quietly and listened, sometimes for two hours or more, before the quickly modulating wail of the sirens sounded the "all clear." When this "all-clear" signal came, I could literally hear people in the shelter let out their breath, as if they'd been holding it the whole time we'd been in there. I'd also hear people thank God that we were all unharmed and could finally go back to bed.

Some nights there were two or three air raids, each lasting for an hour or two. Thus, most of our supposed "sleeping" hours on such nights were spent sitting up in the basement.

The shelter was only about fourteen feet by eighteen feet, and, with roughly fifty people crammed into it, it really felt small. The adults sat on simple benches, which were built on three sides of the room, away from the door. Children sat on their suitcases by their parents. We kept the door open for ventilation. Nevertheless, we didn't get much fresh air into the room, and what little there was quickly became stale.

Some people stood along the wall, close to the door where there were no seats or benches. Others sat cross-legged on the floor in the middle of the room. And of course, there were those who would go upstairs to look outside from time to time. Naturally, when they returned to the shelter, they were barraged with questions about what was going on up there.

When the air-raid sirens first started going off that autumn, there were no actual attacks on Munich. Apparently the planes, that were thought to be headed for us, ended up going after other targets. As a result, a kind of light-heartedness began to develop among us, a feeling that maybe we weren't ever going to be bombed. This feeling gave rise to us singing and the children started playing and having fun with each other in the shelter.

But soon the sirens began to go off more frequently, and it was clear that Munich was, indeed, being bombed. Sometimes we were lucky and the planes simply flew over us en route to other places. On such nights we would be out of the shelter in half an hour. Nevertheless, the bombings quickly became nerve-wracking, and everyone seemed to be living on about half their usual amount of sleep.

★ ★ ★

Eventually, my aunt and uncle decided that it was best for us to spend more time at Villa Waldeck, since it was many miles from the city and, therefore, the threat of bombings. Indeed, once we were in the country, instead of running for the cellar whenever we heard the sound of Allied planes, Aunt Rosa and I hurried upstairs to her bedroom window or even walked to the church to actually *look* for the bombers!

As part of my aunt's work we were looking, not for bombs, but for another kind of object falling from the sky: external fuel tanks from Allied aircraft.

Agnes in the Alps watching for planes.

127

These large metal cylinders, measuring about six to eight feet long, were routinely dropped by bombers on long-distance runs when they needed to carry extra fuel. But Allied intelligence often purposely dropped empty tanks as a way of marking the areas where their agents had parachuted out – usually from the same airplane.

Whenever Aunt Rosa received word that such an operation was taking place near St. Margarethen, we watched carefully for the tank drop. We then walked out into the night, our way illuminated by starlight, until we reached the area where we expected the fuel tank to be. We sometimes used an enclosed candle or petroleum lantern to find the empty cylinder. Once we located it, we would try to make contact with the agent or agents who had parachuted in.

Fortunately, St. Margarethen was a farming community; thus most of the people went to bed early, so they could get up at dawn. What was more, the trees and hills made it difficult for any of the locals to spot us during our rescue operations. Unfortunately, they also made it harder for us to find our underground agents. Sometimes, it took us *days* to do so.

I remember a time when nearly half a week passed before we could locate an Englishman, who had broken his arm during his jump from an Allied plane. We had to keep him hidden in our secret room at the Villa Waldeck, so that he had time enough to rest and let his arm mend.

About two weeks later we took him over the mountain to his next destination. A woman agent and I became his instant "family." She assumed the role of his wife and I became their child. Such family groups

always attracted less suspicion if we encountered anyone along the way. It took us six hours to go up the
mountain and point the Englishman to his next stop
en route out of Germany. We stayed overnight in a
forest. The next day we, the "family," returned to St.
Margarethen, but without the "father." Happily, we
were later informed that he made it back to England
three weeks after our trip up the mountain with him.

Shortly after we returned to the villa, the
woman agent left for Berlin to carry out another
assignment. And a few days later I was given a new
agent number with new responsibilities. Although I
no longer received all of my assignments and directions through my aunt, I continued to depend on her
to help me, whenever there was a question to be
answered or a decision to be made.

Much of my new work involved delivering
messages. As before, I rarely understood their subjects. My job was simply to execute the procedures for
communicating securely and accurately the information I was given. Meeting these two goals sometimes
meant that my timing wasn't always perfect in delivering the messages. But it was more important to get the
message to the right person and to do it without being
seen in one place for too long, or being spotted in that
place more than once.

I felt comfortable coming and going during day-
light hours, when I could see where I was and who
was around me. But, at night, I was very edgy when
going to meet my contacts. Part of this came from a
talent I'd developed, a sort of sixth sense, for always
looking over my shoulder without actually turning my
head. Naturally, if I'd ever indulged the impulse to

stop and turn around when I suspected I was being watched or followed, it might have tipped someone off that I wasn't just a teenage girl walking home from school or going to the market. So I had to use others senses, besides sight, to determine whether I was being followed, and I quickly learned that very careful listening was an important part of developing this skill.

For example, I learned to listen to all of the footsteps around me, so I could hear if someone's gait was changing to keep pace with the changes in my own. If I heard this happening, I would know it was too risky to try to meet my contact. This part of my defenses was so important that I wore no metal cleats or protectors on the soles of my shoes. I couldn't allow anything to interfere with my ability to hear.

If I sensed that someone was following me, then saw the same person reflected in a window I passed, I would duck into a crowd of people or a busy store, which I knew had more than one entrance or exit. My small size was a big help with this, especially in a crowd, where I could literally disappear, surrounded by so many other taller people. When this happened, my heart began to race and I would say a silent prayer, asking God to let me get away and return home safely. But I had to be careful not to let my fear make me walk faster, appear nervous or otherwise betray me. And all of these skills seemed more difficult to utilize at night, than during the day.

To hail my contact, I would often whistle four notes from a well-known tune. The words to the notes were *herzie-puppe,* or "heart-doll," meaning "doll of my heart or my beloved". My contact was listening for someone whistling these notes and would respond to me with code words which confirmed that he or she was the right person for me to address. I would then speak briefly to him or her, using the exact words in the precise order in which I'd received them. As I passed on this information, my sixth sense was always operating. If, at any time, I got the feeling that something was not right, I would break off, even in the middle of a message.

Often, after making a successful contact, I had company most of the way home in the form of refugees I was rescuing. That made me feel much better, especially at night.

I remember one occasion when such an assignment kept me out until after dawn. Unfortunately, my uncle couldn't sleep on that particular night and he heard me sneak into the apartment at about 5:00 a.m. Naturally, he questioned me about keeping such hours, especially given the Nazis' curfew; and all I could tell him was that I had been out doing some work for Aunt Rosa. Later in the morning, when my aunt awoke, Uncle was furious with her.

"Rosa! What, in the name of Heaven, is a young child like Agnes doing staying out until all hours of the morning? This is outrageous!"

It was rare that Uncle Georg would confront my aunt, but I was his "favorite" niece and I think he was worried – and a little suspicious – that my aunt was doing something that was pushing me too hard and placing me in harm's way.

Some time later, my uncle again caught me coming in late from an assignment, this time when we were staying out at the villa. Fortunately, Aunt Rosa was awake this time and her ability to improvise came immediately into play. Half-asleep, on the spur of the moment, she convinced my uncle that I had not been out all night. "No, no, Georg. I sent Agneška down early to empty the chamber pot. The chamber pot."

This explanation seemed to satisfy Uncle; but I think he still had a feeling that there was more going on than met the eye – that Aunt Rosa was up to something. After that, he kept asking me, "Agnes, are you getting enough sleep? You look tired and worn out. Is everything all right? You should lie down for a half hour when you get home from school, so you don't get sick."

I really appreciated my uncle's concern and it was nice to know he cared about me. But the naps he recommended weren't always possible, because there were messages to be delivered after school, too. Fortunately, Uncle was usually at his office during those hours. So sometimes I napped, but usually I didn't.

★ ★ ★

Most Sunday afternoons in 1943 and early 1944, my sister Rosa and I visited my sister Mila at a home in the Munich suburb of Pasing, where Mila worked as a cook and housekeeper. She was employed by a retired couple. The husband, a man in his mid-60s, had been a school teacher of students in their early teens. Both he and his wife were good friends of my aunt and uncle. In fact, it was through that connection that Mila had gotten the job.

She loved working for the couple. They were quite kind to her, giving her room and board, which made it possible for her to send money back home to

Paderovce to help our parents. The retired school teacher and his wife also allowed Mila to have Rosa and me come to visit each week and feed us delicious cake and coffee. All three of us sisters always had a lot of fun talking and joking, but, for me, the trips to and from Pasing were also occasions for work.

The Munich streetcars made excellent places for contacting other agents and exchanging messages. It also helped that our visits to my sister Mila always followed a fairly tight schedule, due to the streetcar connections. Rosa and I had Sunday lunch at Aunt and Uncle's apartment at 12:00. Then we caught the 1:00 streetcar and arrived in Pasing at about 1:30 to visit Mila. After our visit, we left at 4:30 sharp.

Usually, I made contact on the streetcar through seemingly incidental conversation. Sometimes I would look at my watch and say, "only five minutes left."

That would prompt my contact or contacts (they were sometimes couples), to say, "Oh, what time do you have?"

And I would give a time that was actually five minutes fast or slow. This told my contact(s) that it was safe to pass on the message. The contact(s) would then ask me what time the streetcar reached a certain stop.

I answered, "Fifteen minutes to two," the coded message for which my contact was waiting.

My contact(s) would then thank me, and that was all we said to each other.

Sometimes my sister Rosa, who saw the time my watch actually displayed, would ask me, "Why did you tell those people the wrong time?" And I would have to make up a story about my watch running slow. More often, however, she would simply comment, as we walked back to the apartment, "We sure met some friendly people today!"

And all I could do was agree with her. It wasn't possible for me to tell her why they were so friendly.

When we got home my aunt would ask us, "How was your afternoon?"

And Rosa answered, "We met the nicest people on the streetcar."

My aunt would tell her, "Be careful about talking to strangers." Then she'd turn to me, offer me a covert wink, and say, "I'm glad you're home and all right." Naturally, she knew all about the espionage contacts on the streetcars.

★ ★ ★

One of my more complicated operations involved Jewish people and French and English prisoners, who were hidden all over and gathered onto a bus one Sunday, along with *German military* personnel! We mixed in our people, who had the right identification to go to France as military re-enforcements, and it worked. We were able to send off seven: three Jewish men, two French officers, and two English sergeants. A couple of days later I was delighted to learn that the operation was a success.

My next assignment was to find an American. I was recruited for it because of my fluency in English. Another couple and I were to pose as a family on a bicycling trip. We sang a certain song that would let the American know we were his contacts. He was trying to get to Austria by following roads paralleling the autobahn, which would bring him close to the villa.

But, after three weeks and numerous attempts to locate him, we hadn't succeeded. Nevertheless, we received word that he was still alive and that we *must* find him.

We had already looked along several roads, and we had to be careful about using the same route too often. The three of us rode our bicycles with the woman in front, looking and listening to the left. I was in the middle, scanning both sides of the road. And the man rode behind me, concentrating on the right side.

Finally, after three days of bicycling, we heard a response to our signal from some woods to the left of the road, about seven kilometers from the villa. The American crept out of his hiding place like a dog getting up from a long, deep sleep. We had been searching for nearly four weeks, and we all thanked the dear Lord that we had finally found him!

He was very tired and hungry, of course, having survived on what little he could steal from nearby farms. He hugged his radio communication box to him, and for good reason. By keeping him in contact with the underground and letting us know he was still out there, that radio had saved his life.

We had some clothes for him to change into, and we gave him some food. We talked in a ditch for about an hour, while he ate hungrily. He said some Germans had given him some food, believing that he was a displaced worker; but, other than that, he'd had little to eat or drink, except for what he had scrounged from the countryside. When it was time to go back to the villa, the man who had ridden out with us, gave the American his bicycle. And because this man was a

German, he was able to hitchhike back to Munich without arousing suspicions.

Again posing as a "family," we bicycled to the villa; but this time I returned with a different "father" than the one with whom I'd left!

After resting for a couple of days, the American, who revealed to us that he was a lieutenant colonel from New York, set up a communication line. He made contact with London and through London, connected to Washington. To my surprise, his message to Washington was, "Biking was fun. Will stay awhile with…," and then he gave them my code number.

I didn't have time to ask him any questions then – even though I had all sorts of things I wanted to ask about America. Instead, I had to return to Munich the next day. But, a week later, I came back to the villa for the weekend. And, at that time, I was finally able to hear all about his family in New York, and, of course, all about the United States. I told him that I hoped I could visit America after the war, and he said he hoped I could, too.

After another week of school in Munich, I returned to the villa the following weekend for more talk with the lieutenant colonel. This time there was work to do. He gave us a date when empty fuel tanks were to be dropped nearby, along with five parachutists. Five of us underground workers had to wait and be Johnny-on-the-spot to locate these men and bring them to the villa, before the Germans could discover them.

At the appointed time, the five of us found the fuel tanks and the parachutists. We gathered up their parachutes, then we left the area in groups of two or three to rendezvous at Villa Waldeck. We quickly buried the silk parachutes in our garden and got the men into our underground room. They stayed there for a few days before leaving on their mission.

I got lots of hugs and kisses from all of them. They just could not believe that such a young girl was involved in so dangerous a mission.

The lieutenant colonel told Aunt Rosa and me that his job was done in our area and that it was time for him to move on.

"I can't thank you enough for saving my life and the lives of so many others. I will never forget you," he said.

Indeed, it had been quite a memorable week for all of us!

★ ★ ★

Toward the end of May in 1944, my fellow underground workers and I enjoyed a week when we were able to get French prisoners into the villa and over the mountains to freedom at the rate of *two a day!* I only made one such weekend trip with some of these prisoners, who were headed for Switzerland and then on to England. (This was because I still had six weeks of school left before summer vacation began.)

We were sorry to hear later that three of these prisoners were shot before they could reach Switzerland. But we also lost one of our own people in this process. This was the first time I heard that one of ours had been killed. What was more, the victim was a man with whom I'd worked for over a year. None of us had a chance to see his body or pay last respects, except in our thoughts and prayers.

By the end of that month, the snow was gone

from the mountains. That meant that we would no longer leave tracks which the Nazis could follow. So now we were trying harder than ever to get as many prisoners out of Germany as possible. But, given the loss of the POWs and our man, the German SS and the mountain troops were reinforced and put on alert. So, for the time being, the mountain route was no longer an option for us.

Instead, we changed our escape route to the trains which ran to Italy. I never got to ride on one, but visited our train station on weekends. I would bring escapees with me from Munich to as far as Degerndorf. There I would make contact with the brother of the man we'd just lost, since he'd agreed to take his sibling's place in our secret work. He would then ride with the POWs on the next leg of the train journey.

Using the trains was actually more dangerous because there were many Nazis aboard them and the escapees had to have forged passports that were convincing enough to get stamped by the border guards. And, if I was traveling with people who didn't speak German, they had to keep silent.

I didn't worry about myself so much on these trips as I did the prisoners I was helping to escape. If one of them slipped up, there was not much I could do to save them. Usually, I would use a finger signal or the wink of any eye to indicate to them when it was safe to speak to me.

While we did succeed it getting some more POWs out via these trains; one of the links in our chain of message relays had been penetrated by the Nazis and it made communication slow and difficult while the chain was being rebuilt. Thus we didn't make as much progress as we would have liked.

★ ★ ★

At the end of June, I finished school with an A- average and received credit for two years of college. The sirens were blowing, but the bombs had not yet begun to fall on the city itself. So far, the Munich area had only been bombed once. And that had been near Dachau, where many Jews were still working and dying in the camp. As tragic as that had been, it seemed that Munich was still fairly safe and our country villa even safer. Nevertheless, my uncle was concerned about my welfare and he told Aunt Rosa that he felt I needed a good rest. My aunt agreed and suggested sending my sister, Rosa and me home to Slovakia for three weeks. My sister and I were delighted. It seemed an entire lifetime had passed since my days in Paderovce.

When our train pulled into Trnava, Slovakia on July 23, 1944, all sorts of thoughts filled my head. Of course, I wondered how my parents and other siblings were getting along. But I was also very curious about the kids I'd grown up with. Would any of the boys I'd once attended school with find me attractive, now that I'd matured? And was it possible for me to get all of my questions about my past classmates answered before Rosa and I returned to Germany on August 13th?

After four long years away from my homeland, I was overjoyed to see my family again. Everyone was still there. Even my brother, Josef, who was now stationed at a Slovak Army base, bicycled the 30 miles from Morova to see Rosa and me!

I also saw my friends Mariska, Yvonna, and Mila. But, my other classmate, Stefina – one of the girls who had dared me to eat dirt in exchange for a straw ring – was jealous of me now for having left my poverty-stricken circumstances and gone on to a more prosperous life in Germany. Thus I was told she was avoiding me, and I never did see her during this homecoming.

As for the boys I'd known in school, I was certainly not the dirty, sickly little kid they all remembered. Now I wore nice clothes – no more babushka! And I had shot up to four feet, eight inches tall. I'd had a nice haircut before leaving Munich, and the boys in town were definitely noticing me. In fact, they came to our home, and I had a date almost every day! Many times we just sat on the bench in front of the house or took a walk through town – which didn't take long, since Paderovce hadn't grown much. Its population was still roughly three hundred, with only about forty eight homes along the main street.

My brother, Josef, wore his uniform with the two stripes, which showed he was a non-commissioned officer. He was very proud of what he'd achieved since leaving Paderovce, and he told me, "See? I'm doing something right!"

Josef and I had several long conversations during the three days he was home. He was very interested in how I was getting along in Munich. I complained a lot to him about what I was doing, though I couldn't say much about the undercover work with Aunt Rosa. I realized just how tired I was, how much pressure I'd been under, and how much danger I had been in. "Josef," I said, "it's so peaceful here, perhaps I won't go back to Munich."

He responded by looking me squarely in the face and laying down the law. "But you're never going to have it nice or good here in Paderovce and neither will I. That's why I left. At least you have a chance in Germany, even with the war. Or maybe even across the ocean. Here you have no chance. Don't be foolish. Tomorrow is August thirteenth, and I will see to it that you get on that train back to Germany!"

I confessed to him that Rosa and I couldn't go back the next day, because we'd changed the dates on our passports from the thirteenth to the eighteenth, so we could stay longer.

Josef looked incredulous. "What? You could go to jail for doing that!"

I got so worried that I began to cry. Perhaps this was also because the visit was now drawing to a close after three weeks of fun and relaxation.

Nevertheless, Josef was true to his word. He put Rosa and me on the train back to Germany. It wasn't easy. He gave me a big hug and said, "Make good use of your languages. You are the smart one in the family."

As I've said, I really didn't want to go back at first. And Rosa wanted to stay, too, which made it all the harder for me. But, as I got on the train and saw the way Josef looked at me, I began to feel that I had grown. And the last thing Josef said to us as we boarded the train was, "Don't look back."

I heard that sentence again and again as the train chugged back to Munich – and the war.

When Aunt Rosa picked us up at the train station, she told us that Munich was soon to be bombed in earnest, and that we would be leaving the city within a week to live at Villa Waldeck indefinitely.

Nevertheless, it was a very long week! We were in the shelter every night, as Munich was, indeed, bombed. Down in the shelter, the bombing sounded like thunder. The mothers and grandmothers among us prayed their rosaries, and, when the rumbling overhead made it clear that we were just about to be bombed, they began to pray all the more loudly.

Meanwhile, Aunt Rosa, by contrast, became crankier and more ornery, as the explosions grew louder and we started to feel the ground shake. She would begin to tell the women who were praying aloud, "Oh, pray quietly to yourself! Don't try to make everyone do what you do!"

It was not that she was anti-religious. In fact, she put fresh flowers in the vase below the crucifix that hung in her apartment each and every day. It was just that she had a real problem with outward displays of emotion.

Someone would suggest that the dozen or so children in the bomb shelter sing to take their minds off their fear. So they would sing folk songs, like the ones I played on the accordion, or even Christmas carols. But Aunt Rosa, who didn't have much patience with small children, would snap at the suggestion, saying, "Ah, they already sang. Let's listen to what's going on outside."

The only thing Aunt Rosa seemed to hate more than listening to the kids sing was hearing them cry. So I truly think there were times when she would rather have been outside, taking her chances with the bombs!

We could tell, by the crackling sound of the huge explosions and by the way the whole shelter vibrated, when bombs were falling close by. At such times, the shelter filled with screams and swearing. The children would cry and the adults would pray at the top of their voices. For our part, however, my sister Rosa and I simply clung to the legs of our aunt and uncle, who usually stood with their backs to the wall.

More than once, when a bomb exploded close by, I heard Aunt Rosa exclaim under her breath, "Jesus, Mary, and Joseph!" – which meant she was about as excited or fearful as she ever got. Many times, after a huge nearby explosion, I felt certain that, in the next moment, the roof of the shelter would come crashing down upon us. Fortunately, Uncle had built it very well, and, after the sirens gave the all-clear signal, we would emerge unscathed, only to see fire raging in the buildings all around us.

But, on the sixth day after we returned from Slovakia, our luck ran out. The sirens called us down to the shelter around midnight and, soon thereafter, the building adjoining ours took a direct hit. Fortunately, our block of buildings, like most in Munich, were made with iron beams and lots of concrete, as well as bricks and mortar. Although our building was still pretty much intact, the door to our shelter had been blocked with rubble. Thus we could not get out that way and we had to use a tunnel which ran through the basements of two adjoining buildings. But, even taking this route, we had to clear rubble to make our way out to the street. Much of this work was done in the dark, because we couldn't use our flashlights until the all-clear sounded.

As we struggled to find our way out of the basement, we could hear the screams and moans of the people who were trapped above and around us. We were all working hard, and Aunt Rosa cautioned us, saying, "That's enough. That's enough. Save yourself. Conserve your strength."

By the time we got out to the street, three hours had passed and it was 3:00 a.m. All of the men from our building were helping to dig out the others in our complex who hadn't been as lucky as we had. Our building itself was not too badly damaged, but the ones next to us were now in disastrous shape.

We never went to bed that night. Aunt Rosa, my sister, and I went back into our building and gathered our belongings, so we could move out to the villa as soon as possible. At nine o'clock that morning, my uncle and two men came with a truck to load our

The Schneiders' apartment building before the bombing. *Same building after the 1943 bombing.*

The neighboring buildings after the bombing.

luggage for the move. Nevertheless, we didn't get out of the city until that afternoon, because Uncle and the other men were still digging for people and bringing them out of the rubble.

It was horrible! Some of those they rescued emerged without arms or legs! And there was blood *everywhere.* There were people crying and clawing through the shattered concrete by hand, in the hopes of finding a buried loved one.

It was not always the bombing that killed people. Heart attacks, caused by fear, took their tolls as well. Our neighbors in the apartment below us, the Wunners, were in the shelter with us that night. When the rest of us got up to leave via the tunnels, they remained on their benches, both of them dead where they sat! I never learned whether this was due to their having suffered heart attacks or strokes. All I could be fairly sure of was that sheer terror had been the real cause behind their deaths.

Later in the morning, a lady was pulled from the rubble, her a face a deep shade of blue, which is a sure sign of cyanosis. As they lifted her out, I heard her exclaim, "I am here. I made it," as she took a deep breath. But it was too much fresh air too quickly for her and she shook and shuddered. Then she threw her arms out straight at her sides, crumpled into a heap, and died on the spot!

It took ten hours to find twenty five people under all the debris. Of these, six were dead and three others died after they got fresh air too quickly. Six more people were recovered in good condition, and the rest had suffered a variety of injuries.

After so many hours of this gruesome work, my aunt said, "We've witnessed and helped enough here. It's time we stay in the country. We are leaving now!"

CHAPTER EIGHT

VILLA WALDECK

In September of 1944, my sister, Rosa started high school. Meanwhile, I had private teachers at the Villa Waldeck. After graduating, I was supposed to go into training to become a nurse, but the sight of blood often made me pass out. My Uncle seemed to think I was faking this response, so he took me to watch a surgical operation, which was performed by a friend of his. Aunt Rosa, who knew I wasn't faking and also wanted me to be available to work with her, told my uncle, "She won't make it. It'll be too much for her." And my aunt was right. About five minutes into the surgery, I fainted to the floor of the operating theater! So much for a nursing career.

Instead, I took a variety of courses in general subjects in which I was already somewhat proficient. These included math, accounting, and languages. Having the teachers come to the villa for my schooling made it much easier for me to do my missions and to help Aunt Rosa with her work. Not surprisingly, my sister came to resent the fact that she had to go out to school, while I had special teachers coming into the house just for me. I'm sure she also sensed that I was my aunt and uncle's favorite. But, because she knew nothing about the work I was doing with Aunt Rosa, she didn't see the down side of that favoritism. And, of course, I could say nothing to her about it.

Now that we were living out at the villa on an ongoing basis, I was available at any time for missions. I really liked living in the country. With the fresh air, the woods, and mountains we could going hiking and enjoy the outdoors any time we wished. I also got to meet more of our neighbors on the nearby farms, as well as the townspeople of St. Margarethen.

I had many contacts at the villa during this period, and we had lots of "guests" in our secret shelter beneath the fruit trees. Most of these guests were French and English, but there were some Americans, too. None of them could stay with us for more than a week, however. This was for their own safety, as well as ours. But it was also because we knew that we would soon need the space for others.

Now, all of this coming and going from the villa might have looked suspicious, if not for the fact that Uncle was having some repair work done around the place. One of his Nazi friends, a general, had arranged for my uncle to use a German Army truck for hauling needs during this reconstruction. He'd also assigned some of his soldiers to the work of repainting and repairing the villa. Therefore, our neighbors grew accustomed to seeing the truck and the soldiers on the grounds.

And thus the scene was set for us to successfully smuggle our secret guests in and out of the villa during daytime hours. Never letting Uncle know about her undercover work, Aunt Rosa simply used his name in order to obtain some German Army uniforms; and these gave our "guests" the perfect disguises for moving freely about the villa. They even mowed the lawn and trimmed the hedges on occasion.

As more and more German men were being drafted into the army, this sort of private repair and maintenance work often fell to *"ausländers,"* especially Russians and Poles. And, fortunately for us and our secret visitors, the German carpenters and other skilled tradesmen would not talk to the lower workers on the grounds, especially the *ausländers,* because of their supposedly inferior status. Thus there was little chance of any of our "guests" being asked to speak in German and thereby having their true identities discovered.

Naturally, this was a very busy period for us. Just about every week, we had people coming and going from the villa at all hours of the day and night. Quite a few airplanes were being shot down over our part of Germany at this time, so we hid many members of those air crews, who had bailed out and eluded capture. Our villa was one of their last underground stops on the way to Switzerland, so they followed certain signals and arrived at our place to find that we had food and clothes ready for them and they could rest up before we sent them on to the next secret stop.

Soon, however, the cold and rain of autumn arrived, causing the outside work on the house to end and the army truck to stop coming to us. Nevertheless, Aunt Rosa would not be deterred by anything as insignificant as a change of season. Because we would be spending the entire winter in the country, we needed lots of wood and coal brought up to the villa. But hidden amidst the woodpile, my aunt saw to it that there was something else: at least twelve pairs of skis, which would enable us to continue to take our "guests" over the mountains throughout the winter.

★ ★ ★

At Christmas, my sister Mila came to the villa for the holidays. We had not seen her for five months and we had a wonderful visit with her. Since the couple she lived with were in a suburb on the edges of Munich, away from the main targets, their house had not been bombed. Nevertheless, Mila told us, the sirens would awaken them nearly every night. They had a bomb shelter to go to, but Mila remarked often during her visit about how peaceful it was out at the villa and that she was happy she did not have to go back to the city for a while.

Sirens would also go off in St. Margarethen, but it was usually because the planes were flying over us on their way to or from other targets. As a result, we never took shelter from bombings while at the villa. Instead, when the sirens went off, especially at night, Aunt Rosa and I would head upstairs to her window to watch for the airplanes and see what they might drop – so we could get to a fuel-tank marker before the German soldiers did. At other times, we walked up to the church in the dark. There, we had a clear view of the surrounding hills, where tanks or men would sometimes be dropped.

We weren't the only ones out and about at that

time, however. So Aunt Rosa would put her acting talent to use. She would play the role of worried and nervous Frau Schneider. "Oh my house, my precious house," she would exclaim to anyone within earshot.

And, considering how beautiful Villa Waldeck was and how many years my aunt had lived there, the locals seemed to believe that she truly was looking at the sky out of fear that it would be bombed.

But, of course, Aunt Rosa and I weren't looking for bombs. Indeed, we were looking for anything *else* that might be dropped from the sky. And, sometimes, what fell were Allied propaganda leaflets. We often picked them up to see what they said. Written in German, they explained that the Americans were coming and that the German people should not be scared. "Hold on," they read, because the war would soon be over.

By this time, most of us realized that Germany could not win the war, and we were wishing it would just come to an end. So, even though it was propaganda, people took the leaflets' claims seriously and most believed them.

More importantly, however, the leaflets served the purpose of drawing the locals' attention away from the more important things that were being dropped: parachuting Allied men and the empty fuel tanks that were meant to mark their locations.

I particularly remember one night at 2:00 a.m., when Aunt Rosa and I heard planes approaching. We got dressed and walked up the hill, until we were about a thousand feet from the villa. Then we turned around and began heading back.

My aunt sensed that we were being followed.

"Hush," she exclaimed in a whisper. "I think someone is walking behind us."

We kept on walking until we reached our gate. Then we stopped and stood quietly looking up at the stars. After about two minutes, we heard a voice behind us repeating my agent number. I answered the voice using some designated code words.

After several seconds, two men came out of some brush on the side of the road and identified themselves to us as American parachutists. We quickly took them into the secret room and got them something to eat and drink. Then we went to bed.

The next morning we went to the secret room and talked to them briefly. They told us where they were from and about the mission they were on. They also claimed that they had tried once before, earlier in the evening, to make contact with us, but had been unsuccessful. They were, nevertheless, very relieved that they'd only had to make two attempts to get to the villa.

Their relief was not to last long, however, because, by mid-morning of that same day, some SS men found an empty fuel tank about two miles up the hill from the villa. In short order, nearly every household within a six-mile radius of the tank received a visit from the SS. They demanded to know if we had seen or heard anything the night before when the Allied planes had flown over St. Margarethen. Of course, we told them we hadn't, and, fortunately, the rest of our neighbors made the same claim. This was probably true, in any case, because our American guests later confirmed for us that they had buried their parachutes in a large hay stack upon landing.

So, all evidence of their drop – short of the empty fuel tank – had been hidden.

Luckily, the SS men seemed to believe us and we were able to hide the Americans for two days before they headed on to Switzerland.

There were others who were not nearly as lucky, however. At about this same time, two French prisoners escaped their work crew and the SS was searching high and low for them. As it turned out, the prisoners had been working for a nearby farmer half days, and, when the SS discovered them hiding in this farmer's fields, they shot them on the spot.

Not too long after that, Aunt Rosa said, "Agnes, I think that the line has gone dead somewhere. Someone way on top must have gotten hit." What she meant was that we had lost a key member in our chain of agents, and, thus, the work of passing people and information out of the country had almost come to a halt. I was wondering why things had been going so slowly for several weeks, and now my aunt had answered that question. In any case, it must have taken some time for the damage to the network to be repaired; and, even once it was, we never did find out exactly what had gone wrong.

But, for me, it was actually worse not to be doing our underground work. Aunt Rosa sent me repeatedly to places – to the store in St. Margarethen, to the local farmer's for milk. And I was always dispatched with the same command: "Go! Look around! See what you can find out!" So, I could only conclude that the lack of activity was even harder on Aunt Rosa, than it was on me.

★　★　★

After my graduation from school, the German government told me I had to work in a factory making gas masks. That definitely didn't sit well with my aunt, because she had other plans for me. Yet there was no way she could get around this order. She had to obey; but, of course, she had no intentions of doing so without a fight. She asked one of my uncle's Nazi friends to look into the matter for us. In the meantime, however, I spent two grueling weeks in the factory. Of course, *ausländers* got the worst jobs wherever they were in Germany; and I was no exception to this. Thus, I got stuck operating big machines, yet I was so short that I had to stand on tiptoes to do so!

Not only was that a dangerous way to work, but it prevented me from even coming close to meeting my production quotas of masks. The penalty for failing to make quota was a couple of lashes, but the supervisor took pity on me because I was so short and he refrained from beating me. Finally, after two weeks which made my undercover work seem like a dream job by comparison, my uncle's Nazi friend came through for us. He managed to obtain the paperwork necessary to get me a work assignment elsewhere.

I was so relieved! I felt as if I'd been freed from slavery. On my last day at the factory, the supervisor, who was supposed to have lashed me for not meeting my quotas, escorted me out of the building. I thanked him for not giving me the lashes, and he said, "Okay, kid. Behave while you are in Germany."

I'm not sure what he would have thought of my behavior as an Allied agent; but my new job, working in the local grocery store, was ideal for the continuance of my intelligence work. This store was only a quarter of a mile from the railroad station and about a 30-minute walk down the hill from our villa. Thus it was the perfect stop-over spot between the train system and our house. The store afforded train travelers their last chance to buy food and supplies before hiking into the mountains. Thus the road outside the store was a heavily trafficked one; and weekends were especially busy, with people coming in from the cities to spend time mountain climbing and skiing. The store did a brisk business selling them bread, butter, and sandwich meats for their hikes into the mountains. So, there I was in the midst of people from outside the area, coming and going in public, yet still so close to the villa.

Aunt Rosa was pleased with my new position, as well. Indeed, it was exactly where she wanted me, because it allowed me to serve as her eyes and ears in town without raising any suspicions. And it was obviously an easy place for me to make contacts.

For three months, the Nazis checked up on me constantly, repeatedly asking the store's owners if I was a good worker. Since the owners, Frau Klepper and her unmarried daughter, Lisl, were my aunt's friends and I did my job well, they naturally told the Nazis as much. But, then again, the Kleppers knew nothing about all the secret communications I had in the store.

I began working there as a *lehrling* (an apprentice), which meant that I did most of the cleaning. I swept the floors, polished the fixtures, and washed the windows. But Aunt Rosa wanted me to be able to talk to and wait on the customers in order to facilitate our underground work, so Frau Klepper also allowed me to weigh food and other supplies for the shoppers.

Frau Klepper was in her sixties and, like Aunt Rosa, she was quite outspoken; so she and I got along fairly well.

Lisl, however, was a different story. She seemed to resent my abilities in the store; and, because of her long nose and short haircut, I used to secretly call her "The Witch." Once, for example, I was helping Frau Klepper glue some bread ration stamps onto their sheet and pre-weighing the bread to match the stamp amounts, when Lisl began vehemently objecting. She didn't think I should be helping with such tasks. She said that, because I was an *ausländer,* I was only fit to do the store's dirty work – the scrubbing, cleaning, and polishing. But, because Frau Klepper was stubborn and authoritative, she didn't like her daughter telling her what to do; so this outburst on Lisl's part practically ensured that I'd spend more time waiting on customers.

There were some other German girls working in the store, too; and I got along very well with them. My best friend among them was Dora. (She and I wrote to each other for many years after the war, and, in fact, she was still working in the store as late as 1966.) In any case, my undercover contacts would sometimes approach Dora or one of the other girls and ask them questions which I recognized as codes. Since the underground workers didn't know who in the store was their contact, they would ask their questions to see if they got the proper response. If I happened to overhear such an inquiry, I'd go over to whomever they were addressing and nod my head, so that the undercover man or woman would realize that I was their contact and the prearranged question wouldn't have to be asked a second time.

Among the most popular items in the store were the delicious hard rolls, which the Germans called *semmel*. Contacts, who were unsuccessful in reaching me when they first came in, could always return without attracting attention by saying that they just had to have one more of those scrumptious *semmel*. When the contact and I were sure of each other, he or she would then ask me, "What time does the store close?" And, depending on my answer, the contact would know when I was free to act further, such as leading him or her up to the hidden room at the villa or giving directions to the next underground stop.

Another code that we used successfully involved the contact asking me, "What's the best route to this mountain? And how long does it take to get there?" At other times, they would ask me the altitude of a certain mountain. The first and the last word in the questions gave me my signal. If it was delivered correctly, I gave the answer, also coded; and I always silently prayed that I was giving it to the right person!

Depending on how they responded to my reply, I knew whether to lead them to our villa. But, because these secret exchanges were going on amidst the bustle of a busy store, I didn't have time to do much thinking. I had to rely almost solely on instinct. And both our questions and responses had to be appropriate for the setting of the store. They also had to be banal enough not to arouse the suspicion of anyone who might overhear them. In addition, many *ausländers* shopped there, so I had to take extra care never to speak anything but German. Using a foreign language would have made me far too suspect.

The store closed about 2:00 p.m. on Saturdays, and I often left with people following me back to the villa at that time. When I reached our gate, I would stop. And, without turning back to look at them, I would say, "Keep on going up the road, then turn around and come in the back in fifteen minutes."

As they walked past, I would hear a whispered, "See you in fifteen minutes." I could tell from their accents whether they were English or Americans.

On nice days, there were many hikers and visitors to St. Margarethen walking up the hill; thus, my contacts could not use the front gate. Rather, they had to sneak in via the back way.

I lost count of how many people we brought through the villa in those final months of 1944.

★ ★ ★

For years, the Nazis had used the large astro-nomical observatory on Wendelstein Mountain for relaying radio messages. It handled strategic and tactical radio traffic with military units in Western Europe, as well as those on the Russian Front. Because of its importance, it was garrisoned with SS, as well as Wehrmacht, troops. One of our men worked under-cover on the Wendelstein observatory. He was our best connection and was a key reason why we used the mountains as a route to get our people out of Germany.

But, about the time of the first snow fall in late 1944, we lost this man at the observatory and we didn't get a replacement for several weeks. As usual, we never found out what happened, but we thanked God that we were notified of the change promptly. Otherwise, we could have found ourselves in great danger, with the SS so feverishly on the lookout for other members of our network. We needed a bit of a break, however, because the pressure had been high for several weeks with so many people coming through. Now, with the loss of our man on Wendelstein, we really couldn't afford any mistakes.

Three weeks passed before the new replacement at the observatory contacted us to let us know that we would be working together. He'd been thoroughly trained to handle relay networks like ours. But we were surprised to learn that he was also able to directly contact Washington, D.C.! Apparently he had a lot of skill changing and reinforcing the cables, antennas, and other wires, as well as making various technical changes at the observatory, because his senior officers were very pleased with his work and had placed him in charge of all communications.

While it seemed to me he was going to be a great help to us, Aunt Rosa was not convinced of it. This was partially due to her suspicious nature, coupled, I'm sure, with her grief at the recent loss of our trusted comrade at the observatory. The fact that this new man had been given so much power also made her dubious of him. "If he's in charge of all communications," she said to me, "he must be a Nazi!"

And, as we continued to discuss the matter, she began to argue with herself, saying, "Of course, I suppose, after losing the first man, we'd have to get someone in that position who had the complete trust of his superiors. In a way, I suppose he's got to be a Nazi, if he's going to be any help to us at all. Still, it makes me nervous."

A couple of weeks after that, our new contact at the observatory was skiing down from Wendelstein and stopped to visit with us. He turned out to be a major in the German Army. He appeared to be in his thirties and told us he spoke four languages. His speech and technical accomplishments indicated that he was very intelligent. Aunt Rosa was clearly impressed with him. And he, in turn, was surprised by and impressed with how young I was.

He took the last cog rail of the day back up to Wendelstein. He was a fine German man, and we were happy to have finally met him. However, we soon found that working with him was both demanding and dangerous. He insisted on accuracy and speed – a difficult combination to achieve in any line of work, but especially in espionage. His reasons for the risks were persuasive, however. He saw that the end of the war was near, and he was pushing to save as many lives as possible.

"In six to eight months, we will all be free," he told us. "So, keep your chins up." And, because he knew much more about the course of the war than we did, we dearly hoped he was right.

He told us he would continue to stop and visit us as a German officer, which would minimize suspicion; and it didn't take long for Aunt Rosa to build up complete trust in him. In many cases, she actually deferred to his judgment, which was remarkable, considering how single-minded and stubborn my aunt was. As soon as I heard her ask him during a visit, "Herr Commandant, what can we do about this problem?" I knew he had earned her respect. He also became a good friend to us.

That Christmas he brought us gifts and thanked us for the work we were doing. "You are taking great chances and risks that are saving the lives of many people," he told us. Then he said that he had a surprise for me. I couldn't image what it might be since he had already given us gifts.

"Agnes," he said, "I have learned that you are registered with the American government in Washington, D.C. under your code number. After the war is over, it will be possible for you to go to America. They will grant you American citizenship for all of the undercover work you have done for them and for the many American lives you have saved."

"She'd better go and see America," Aunt Rosa interjected. "There's nothing for her here or back in Slovakia."

The major spent a couple of days with us over the holidays. He liked the villa a lot. He was especially impressed with the secret room in the basement. And, as he left, he gave Aunt Rosa a compliment that made her eyes sparkle. "Frau Schneider, if things get tough up on the mountain and I have to leave my station in a hurry, I hope you will let me stay in this hideout. This is the best."

After he left, my aunt reminded me of what the tarot reader in Munich had read in the cards when I'd arrived in Germany five years earlier. Aunt Rosa was absolutely adamant about me going to America after the war. "Oh, my God, child, *Jesu Maria!* Everything the cards said is coming true! They said you will be crossing the ocean, and now you are about to receive the opportunity. You better make the most of it, or you will have me to answer to!"

Aunt Rosa's determination on this score was quite an incentive for me, and I needed all the incentives I could get to make it through the very trying final months of World War II!

CHAPTER NINE

AUNT ROSA'S ARREST

The first couple of months of 1944 were bad. The bombing in and around Munich was intense. It seemed that not a night went by without the heavy drone of bombers overhead. Many people from the city, who had been bombed out of their homes, were being moved to the country to find housing. Out in St. Margarethen, the police went from house to house to see how many rooms were available for these displaced city-folk. At the Villa Waldeck we had a big house in a beautiful location and room enough to take in at least two or three families. But, because we had no running water or bathrooms on our second and third floors, my aunt was able to talk the police into sending us no more than two, childless couples.

Aunt Rosa and I both became concerned about how we would be able to continue our operations with strangers living in the villa. Fortunately, however, our friend at the observatory on Wendelstein understood the situation and came to our rescue. He talked to the mayor of the town and told him that he needed a couple of rooms for his officers and supplies and that he felt the Villa Waldeck was ideal for these purposes. Of course, no officers ever arrived, so we were able to continue our undercover work without interruption. At least for a while.

★ ★ ★

In the middle of March, a car drove up to the villa. I was horrified to see two SS officers and their wives get out and come to the door. When Aunt Rosa answered it, one of the women told her, "We like your house very much. The location is quite beautiful, and we need to get out of the city within the week. Things have gotten very bad there. Could we see what accommodations you have inside?"

"There is no way I will let you into my house," Aunt Rosa bluntly replied, shutting the door.

I was frightened because the officers and their wives looked very angry. But their anger was nothing compared to my aunt's. Nevertheless, I couldn't help wondering if she hadn't gone too far this time.

And, indeed, it turned out that she had! A couple of hours later, one of the SS wives came back to the villa with a German policeman. She demanded that Aunt Rosa let her in, so that she could see the available rooms. When my aunt heard the policeman call the woman "Miss," instead of "Mrs.," she became livid.

"I will not have an SS whore living in my house," she exclaimed to the policeman, again slamming the door in our visitors' faces.

I was speechless! Even Aunt Rosa realized she'd overshot her bounds this time.

"Child, I am afraid that I am in for it now," she admitted. And how right she was!

Two hours later, the Nazi woman was back with two policemen who announced that they were placing my aunt under arrest!

"I want you to know," the woman said indignantly, "that I am a lady, and I am engaged to be married to a high-ranking SS officer."

For once, Aunt Rosa showed the good sense to hold her tongue. In fact, her only utterance was to give me a phone number to call in Munich – as the policemen led her off to their car. It was my uncle's work number, but it was also a code that told me exactly what to do: "Get in the house. Lock the doors. Let no one in, and call Uncle Georg immediately."

And that's exactly what I did, even before the police car pulled out onto the road.

The Nazi woman had come in her own car, and I saw through the window that she had stayed behind. As soon as the police left with my aunt, she was ringing the doorbell again and shouting for me to let her in. But I remembered Aunt Rosa's instructions, and I didn't go anywhere near the door.

My lack of response prompted hear to start calling me names. "You will be joining your mother in jail," she hollered.

I, meanwhile, telephoned my uncle in Munich and told him the whole story, and he said he would be home on the six o'clock train. His tone indicated that he was worried, yet not particularly surprised by what had happened.

After the Nazi woman had given up trying to get in to see the house and finally driven away, I went down to the train station in Brannenburg to meet Uncle Georg.

"We are not going to the jailhouse," he said in greeting, "because I cannot bail her out. My friend in the Party won't be available to help us until tomorrow. We'll have to let her stay overnight. Maybe this will teach her to keep her mouth shut. All we can do is go home and wait."

The next morning, Uncle met his Nazi friend at 9:00 a.m. at the jail in Rosenheim. When they went to the front desk and explained that they were there to bail out Frau Schneider, the guards looked greatly relieved.

"You can have her," one of them exclaimed to my uncle. "She's been nothing but trouble from the moment they brought her in. She was yelling and banging her shoes on the cell bars all night long. If you're married to her, you have our sympathy!"

But, once the guards saw the signature of my uncle's friend, who was a very highly-placed Nazi official, they made no further remarks and Aunt Rosa was released immediately.

Uncle's friend left for Munich, and my aunt and uncle came home. I was happy to see them both, but Aunt Rosa was very tired, after her sleepless night in jail, so she went straight to bed. And, as Uncle and I ate lunch a short time later, he told me, "Maybe next time we won't be able to get Rosa out of the jail. I hope she learned not to insult people. We can't always say what we think. We have to be very careful. Especially now."

By mid-afternoon my aunt was all rested and again ready for a fight. "I'm getting even with the SOBs who put me in jail," were the first words she said when she came back downstairs.

This worried me, especially after Uncle's admonition at lunch. But nothing specific came of her threat. Rather, I think she got even by continuing to do her underground work. I also think that the major on Wendelstein played a big role in cooling her temper after the jail episode. She had great respect for him and he for her. And I am sure he didn't want to lose such a valuable resource.

★ ★ ★

Not long after Aunt Rosa's night in jail, we were well underway with our undercover operations again. One morning, my aunt said to me, "I'm getting Uncle to go with me to visit some friends this afternoon. This is our contact day, and you have to take care of things here. I don't want Uncle Georg to see or hear anything. We'll be having dinner there and should be home by 10:00 p.m. You'll know what to do."

When the messenger arrived at 8:00 that evening, my sister Rosa and I were doing our homework. The code he gave me said that three Americans in German uniforms were on their way to the villa. My sister went to bed about an hour later; but, when the Americans still hadn't shown up by 9:30, I started to worry. What if Uncle Georg came back before they arrived?

Fortunately, I didn't have to deal with that problem, because, just fifteen minutes later, our secret visitors arrived. But, instead of three Americans, there were *six* of them for me to hide — three in German uniforms and three in street clothes.

I rushed them to the underground room, where food and coffee were waiting for them; and I had just come up from the underground room, when Aunt and

Uncle unlocked the front door.

"Is everything okay?" my aunt asked. "Is Rosa in bed?"

I said yes to both of these questions.

"Good," she replied. "You'd better go to bed now, too."

I, in turn, told Aunt Rosa that I wanted to get up at six o'clock the next morning.

"What for?" my uncle asked. "We'll get you up at 7:00. At your regular time."

"Okay," I answered.

My aunt nodded in response to this, and I knew she had gotten my message: getting up at 6:00 a.m. meant that we had six "guests" in the basement.

The next morning, my uncle left for Munich at 8:30. Aunt Rosa made breakfast for the six men and took it down to them. When she came back upstairs, she didn't say anything and neither did I, because my sister had just come down to the kitchen. Unfortunately, she didn't have school that day, so we needed to get her out of the house.

"Rosa, please go to the bakery and grocery store and pick up these items," Aunt Rosa told her; and, as soon as my sister left to run these errands, my aunt and I went down to the underground room to talk to the Americans.

The three men in street clothes had already been in Germany for three weeks and had been very difficult for the undercover network to locate. But they'd been lucky, because one of them spoke German.

The next day we were able to sneak two of them out of the villa and send them on to their next underground stop; and the other four men left a couple of days after that.

Since I was on a week's vacation from the store, I was busy making contacts from home. I was constantly coming and going on my bike, in an effort to find out how soon the Americans would be marching in to occupy our town. I had heard rumors that it would be the first week in June, but no one really knew. The bombing around Munich had become very heavy, and we had gotten word that the ships of the German Navy were ready to retreat into Bremen and Hamburg. It was clear that the war was finally coming to an end.

★ ★ ★

One Friday in May, Uncle Georg came out to the villa for the weekend, and, as he came in the door, I heard him tell my aunt, "Rosa, the war is over. The last air raids on Munich were very bad. They destroyed the Nazi building, and Herr Kolber, my friend who got you out of jail, was killed."

I was very happy to hear that the war had finally ended, but I didn't let it show. We'd all had to hide our true feelings so much during Hitler's reign, that I'd simply gotten into the habit of repressing anti-Nazi sentiments.

★ ★ ★

About the ninth of May, tanks, trucks, and jeeps began pouring through Degerndorf. Hundreds of American GIs marched in along with the vehicles. As all of this was going on, Aunt Rosa sent me to the store to get some supplies. As usual, I brought a bag with two empty bottles in it, so that I could fill them with vinegar and oil at the store.

To my surprise, I encountered four American

soldiers en route. Three of them were white and one was black, and they were pointing their rifles at people and laughing. I had never seen a black person before that day, and that, combined with their dangerous gun brandishing, really put me on edge.

I must have been shaking, because the empty bottles in my bag started rattling when they stopped me.

"You got schnapps in there?" the black soldier asked.

As he looked into my bag and saw the empty bottles, he also noticed the ring and the watch I was wearing. He got his companions to point their guns at my chest, while he took my ring and my watch from me. Then, laughing again, the four of them walked away. After they had gotten about ten feet from me, I passed out right where I stood, on the grass next to the road!

People were so busy greeting the American GIs and talking to them, that no one noticed me or came to help. It must have taken about an hour for the troops to pass through town. And, about that time, I began to regain consciousness. Some of the locals finally spotted me as I slowly got back to my feet and they came to my aid. Eventually, two of our neighbors escorted me home, even though I was only a ten-minute walk from the villa.

These neighbors saw me into the house and told my aunt what had happened to me. As they were talking to her, I again passed out in the entryway!

When I woke up, Aunt Rosa stood beside my bed. "It's about time you woke up, Sleeping Beauty," she said.

She went on to tell me that a doctor had been to the villa to examine me as I'd slept and that I'd been unconscious for about fifteen hours. I'm still not sure exactly why I passed out; but, strangely enough, in all the years of my work as an underground agent and all the high-risk, life-and-death situations I was involved in, I had never had a gun pointed right at me. And stranger still was the fact that the first people to threaten me in that manner were on the very side that I had been risking my life for! It was absolutely the *last* thing I'd expected to have happen, so it was probably shock that caused me to keep fainting dead away – but it was probably also four years of stress being released all at once. Whatever the reason, however, it certainly was a peculiar way to end the war.

Aunt Rosa was glad that I was okay, and, naturally, so was I.

"Now we can rest up," my aunt said. "We certainly did a good job. We lived in danger, but now we can look ahead and won't need to worry about our backs."

★ ★ ★

After a week's rest, I went back to work at the store, but not for long. After the Americans took occupancy of the German barracks and the officers' hotel, they began to search for an interpreter. A German-speaking American lieutenant asked the mayor of St. Margarethen if he knew anyone in town who could speak German and English. Well, he knew a couple of students who went to college, but he didn't know if they'd learned enough English to make good interpreters. After visiting the two students and concluding that they weren't fluent enough in English,

the mayor, along with the German-speaking lieutenant and a lieutenant colonel, knocked at the door
of the Villa Waldeck. They told my aunt what they
were looking for and that this was their third stop. She
invited them in and called for me to come and meet
them. When I saw the two Americans in uniform, I
welcomed them in English.

While Aunt Rosa visited with the mayor, I spoke
at length to the two Americans in their native tongue.
I must have made a good impression on them,
because the lieutenant colonel immediately explained
the needs for the barracks and gave me a list of my
new duties. Then he told me that their jeep, its driver,
and Lieutenant Johnsoner would be available to help
me with whatever I needed to do my work as an
interpreter. It had to have been one of the shortest
job interviews in history!

Before he left the villa, the lieutenant colonel
said almost apologetically to my aunt, "She is so
young. The job is so big. And I'm asking so much – "

"Don't worry," Aunt Rosa interrupted. "She may
be young and small, but, let me tell you, she is a
mighty mouse!"

★　★　★

We had just three days to clean up the barracks
and the converted building in Degerndorf, so the
American troops could move into them. This meant
that I had to recruit a lot of Germans to do the job.
The mayor was a big help with this. In fact, he had
about thirty people ready to work for us the very next
day! The clean-up of the barracks went fine, and the
officers' quarters were soon ready, as well.

It turned out that our new neighbors were the

men of the U.S. 39th Infantry. But, no sooner had they gotten settled in, than the lieutenant colonel had to leave for another German city, in order to get accommodations arranged for more U.S. troops.

Lieutenant Johnsoner and I worked together for about two weeks, so I got to know him fairly well. His parents had left Hamburg, Germany in 1938 to emigrate to the United States. He was about fourteen years old at the time and his family was Jewish. He told me that his parents were very wise to leave Germany when they did. They foresaw the coming holocaust, when many other Jews did not.

He received his American citizenship in 1940 and had enlisted in the Army as soon as he was old enough. Because he spoke fluent German, the Army was happy to have him. In fact, he had been specially trained to be with the first group of occupation troops to arrive in Bremerhaven.

I, in turn, told him about some of the underground work that I had done. He was surprised and said, "I knew we had agents all over, but I didn't think we had one as little as you."

I told him that some of the agents had called me a "mighty mouse."

He laughed heartily and said, "In the two weeks that I've been working with you, I can see that you sure get around and get things done; so I guess the name really fits you."

★ ★ ★

For three or four weeks, U.S. troops were constantly passing through Degerndorf. They would rest a couple of days or a week in the barracks and then leave. Right on their heels, new troops would arrive and take over the barracks. Then the tempo of the troop movements slowed, and, after about six months, it came to an end and the last batch of troops settled in for a much longer stay.

The USO and Red Cross set up facilities during the summer, and, by September, we had three clubs. These included the enlisted men's (EM) club, the non-commissioned officers' (NCO) club, and the officers' club. I helped manage the officers' club, along with two sergeants, Charlie and Frank, who were both chefs. I hired a German chef and all the kitchen help that we needed, as well as waiters.

Agnes walking past the Officers' Club. The base was in background, behind the fence and bare trees.

All of the enlisted men ate at the mess hall on the base. They had their dances and parties at the EM and NCO clubs, which were located off-base. The officers had all their meals at the club and most of their parties, too. That meant freshly cooked meals every day, so keeping the kitchen stocked was a never-ending chore. I would go with one of the sergeant/chefs to translate for them while they did their shopping for fresh meat and vegetables – usually on the black market. Instead of German currency, we used cartons of cigarettes, boxes of candy, and bags of sugar to buy what we needed. Once, for example. we purchased a cow for five cartons of cigarettes, three boxes of O'Henry candy bars, and ten pounds of sugar.

For almost a year, this was how we did most of our shopping for the officer's club. By late 1946, however, most of the fresh foods began to come in from the United States, so the black market slowed down quite a bit. But we could still use cigarettes and candy to buy just about anything we needed.

★ ★ ★

During the spring of 1947, Lieutenant Colonel Stone told me that, for ten days, only a skeleton crew would be left in the barracks, along with a few officers. The rest of the troops were going on a one-hundred-mile hike, as part of an exercise. When the troops returned, I had arranged a big party for them, with plenty of food and liquor.

The manager from the EM club hadn't gotten prepared like I had, so I wasn't too surprised when he called me at noon on the day the troops were due back and told me that he needed my help. Fortunately, I had enough supplies to promise him two-hundred pounds of ground beef, German beer, and about ten cases of liquor. Without them he would have had several hundred very hungry – and unhappy – soldiers to deal with!

I told him I would arrive at the EM Club at 8:00 p.m. – along with my bill, so I could make sure my bookkeeping was kept up-to-date. But the truth of the matter was, that I was less interested in supervising the delivery than I was in finding out which of the local girls would be at the club that evening.

My driver dropped me off at the club at 8:00 p.m. sharp, and I told him to return for me by 9:30 p.m. As I walked into the club, the manager was sitting with six soldiers, who were seated at a table near the door. He introduced me to each of the men in turn.

The club was packed, and many of the girls from town were already dancing and having fun. Thus, it didn't take long before some of the guys from that table started asking me to dance, too. The sixth soldier, who had been introduced to me as Willard Daluge, took his turn at asking me to dance. But, as we were walking to the dance floor, he admitted that he didn't know how to dance. I was so embarrassed that I turned around and walked out of the club!

I couldn't believe he'd do such a thing to me with so many people watching, and I was simply too humiliated to stay! I ran about five-hundred feet across the club's parking lot. Then one of my feet plunged down into the earth and I fell forward. Someone had forgotten to put the cover on a sewer hole, and I had stepped right into it! My right leg was submerged in it all the way over my knee. Now, I wasn't just embarrassed, I was positively mortified!

Fortunately, Willard felt badly about his faux pas, so he'd followed me when I left the club. And this was a blessing, because I definitely needed his help to get me out of the sewer hole! I'd lost a shoe in my fall and my right leg was badly bruised. But far worse was what the fall had done to my pride!

Because it was only about 9:00 p.m., the Officers' Club was still open and I knew I could take refuge there.

Once we reached the gate of the Officers' Club, I told him, "Thank you, and I hope I never see you again!" With that, I headed off to the back room of the club to get cleaned up.

But now Willard knew where I worked. And he also found out that I had a jeep and a driver, who took me all over the area. Occasionally, I would see Willard walking as I was being driven home to the villa, but I never thought that he would figure out where I lived. I don't know how long it took him, but one afternoon I arrived home at about four o'clock to find him sitting at the dining-room table, having coffee and apple pie with my aunt!

"Herr Daluge has been here waiting for you for nearly an hour now, Agneška," Aunt Rosa said in greeting.

I spoke English to him, and they were not very kind words either, but he would not leave. Although she couldn't understand English, my aunt could tell from my tone that I was not being very nice to him. So I explained to her how I met him and why I was so upset.

She said, "But that's my boy. I call him 'Buby.'"

Well, "Buby" or not, I didn't want to see him or have anything further to do with him!

But he didn't seem to get the message. He was constantly coming to the villa to visit my aunt. He brought her cigarettes, candy, American coffee, and of course, whiskey. He spoke German, so my aunt had a wonderful time conversing and drinking with him.

After a couple of weeks, Aunt Rosa said, "He's a nice, quiet boy, Agneška. You should give him a chance. He's not like some of the officers you bring home. And he's not a Chicago gangster, you know."

She suggested that the three of us go to a German movie. Eventually, I gave in and went with her and Willard to see a film, and, before I knew it, this became a regular event. Every Monday night, the three of us went out to see a movie.

Finally, I got up enough courage to overcome my embarrassment and go back to the EM Club to dance. One of the base officers, a Lieutenant Henshaw, saw me go to the EM Club and called me into his office for a talk. "Why are you going dancing at the EM club when there are plenty of officers who are interested in you? Especially *me*."

Well, he was Willard's boss in the radio-com-munications unit, and he made it clear he also didn't like me dating a T-4. Indeed, to show how much he didn't like it, he began giving Willard extra duty and taking away his passes, so that he couldn't leave the barracks.

This went on for about ten days. But Lieutenant Henshaw forgot that I had a pass to go in and out of the base with my reports from the club at any time. Thus, Willard and I were still able to see each other whenever we wished.

That really got Henshaw mad, so he reported me to Major Surahan, who gave me a fatherly lecture. "Why do you want to date an enlisted man, when you could have your pick of the officers?"

Because I couldn't stand Lieutenant Henshaw

and I was angry about him reporting me to the Major, the mighty mouse in me came to the surface again. "Major Surahan," I said, "I don't look at the shiny bars on the shoulders; I listen to the heart."

He seemed to understand this, and he said nothing more on the subject.

A couple of days later, Colonel Stone and his wife also had a talk with me. "Agnes, you do so much for all the American military personnel and their families here. They all like you very much and you are an important part of our operation. So, what's all this about Lieutenant Henshaw?"

"The Lieutenant is harassing me, and he's giving Willard extra duty and taking away his passes, just because he is seeing me. I don't think it's right or fair."

Well, I could see they were taken aback; but they told me something would be done about it soon. And they were true to their word. Within a few days, Major Surahan told me that Lieutenant Henshaw had been transferred to Berlin by helicopter. Because of the Berlin Blockade, this was the only way to get into Berlin – which was, fittingly enough, not a very pleasant duty station.

Agnes sitting in front of the Officers' Club – 1946.

I, meanwhile, continued working for the officers in our town. Most of them and their wives knew that

I had a boyfriend and that he was only a T-4; but they still invited me to all their parties, because they depended on me to get things done.

★ ★ ★

On my birthday in March, 1948, Aunt Rosa told me in her usual blunt way, "You should marry Buby."

"Absolutely not," I replied. "I can go to America without marrying *anyone,* because the government granted me U.S. citizenship for my spy work during the war."

"Agneška, you are only twenty years old and you had better listen to me, because I know what is good for you. Marry Buby." And then, in typical Aunt Rosa fashion, she just went ahead and told Willard, "You can marry Agnes. You have my blessings."

Well, before I knew it, the two of them were planning the wedding for July 15, 1948! I wore Aunt Rosa's wedding dress, which was altered greatly to fit my much smaller frame, and

Agnes' and Willard's wedding, July 15, 1948.

180

we had a beautiful wedding at the Villa Waldeck.

But we began our honeymoon in a somewhat unusual fashion – by hitchhiking! We hitchhiked from Degerndorf to Bad Reichenhall. From there, we went to catch the cable car that took us up to the Predigstuhl, where the hotel was located. It was a beautiful day, and we spent the afternoon walking and admiring the scenery. We could see a storm over the Chiemsee, a lake on which Mad King Ludwig of Bavaria built his fabulous castle in the mid-19th century. We could also look back all the way to the Inntal and Munich.

The hours just flew by. And, by the time we realized how late it had gotten, the wind had begun to pick up. We were going to take the cable car down the mountain, but they had stopped running it, because the heavy winds were causing the car to swing violently back and forth. The operator explained to us that, if the car were to go down the mountain in such winds, it would be smashed against the pylons that held up the cables and that would damage the car, the cables or both.

So we had to stay in the hotel overnight. We were relieved to learn that its staff was prepared for unexpected guests. Apparently it was not at all unusual for people to be stranded on the mountain by the wind. So we went to our room to clean up. Then we had a good dinner, did some dancing and went to bed at about eleven o'clock.

When we got up in the morning, Willard opened the shutters, looked out the window, then called me to come and see the beautiful scenery. When I peered out, I realized our room was hanging right on the edge of the mountain and we could see straight down for hundreds of feet! It was rather scary.

The flowers were blooming all over the sides of the mountains. In fact, when we were out hiking later that morning, Willard held me by my ankles so I could hang over the edge of a sheer drop and pick some alpen roses, which were growing on the side of a cliff.

Afterwards, we took the first cable car down the mountain and back to Bad Reichenhall. Then we hitchhiked to Berchtesgaden, where we spent several days. Hitler's infamous "Eagle's Nest" was located above Berchtesgaden, and he had reached it by an elevator which ran right up through the mountain itself! In Berchtesgaden we had the opportunity to listen to the popular jazz drummer, Gene Krupa and his band.

When it was time to go home, we decided that we had had enough of standing by the side of roads and riding in bumpy "deuce-and-a-half" army transports, so we took the train, rather than hitchhiking again.

When I got back to the Army base, the staff told me how much they'd missed me while I was honeymooning, and it felt very good to know I was so appreciated!

Shortly after we got home, Willard put in a request to go back to the States. It was granted fairly quickly and we soon found ourselves scheduled to leave Germany in mid-October of 1948.

I gave my notice to my employers at the base at the end of August. That was a sad day for me, but a happy one, as well, because I was starting to look forward to a new life in America.

The officers wives gave me a going-away party and lots of good advice. Aunt Rosa was happy for me, yet sad that she was losing me.

★ ★ ★

On October 17, 1948, Willard and I boarded the train and left for Bremerhaven. Two days later, we set sail for the United States on board the *U.S.S. General Gaffney.*

CHAPTER TEN

SECRET AGENT TO WAR BRIDE

The *General Gaffney* was a huge troop ship with hundreds of war brides, their husbands, and even some children aboard. For the husbands, this was a welcome and long-awaited journey. But, for the foreign-born wives, like me, it meant uncertainty and change. We were facing a very new and different life in the land which we had held in our imaginations for so long – the United States of America.

What made this process even more difficult for us was the fact that we were forced to live apart from our husbands during the voyage. The men stayed in crowded and cramped crew holds on the lower decks and they were fed together in a mess hall.

We women, meanwhile, were assigned to cabins on the upper decks. Our rooms were pretty comfort-able, but we, too, were living in crowded conditions – with as many as four of us assigned to a single cabin. We were, however, granted the luxury of eating in the dining room, where we would sit, ten to a table, with a waiter and a menu to order from. Nevertheless, this didn't make up for being separated from Willard.

But, after meals, we were allowed to meet with our spouses on the deck, in one of the lounges, or even in the ship's movie theater. At midnight, however, the men had to go back to their quarters below.

Because I was one of the few people on board who could speak both English and German, I was kept quite busy translating for the other passengers. That helped time to go by quickly. But one very eerie scene still sticks in my memory. It was the sight of numerous torpedoed-ship masts sticking up from under the water, as we passed through the shallow portions of the North Sea and the English Channel. It was a very real reminder of the war.

For several days during our crossing, the seas became quite rough. In fact, they were so choppy that we were told that the huge propellers of the ship were often exposed as the vessel crested the top of the enormous Atlantic waves. In the dining room, some of the children traveling with their parents took the opportunity to slide across the slick wooden dance floor, back and forth with the pitching and rolling of the ship. Of course, this same motion of the vessel wasn't at all fun for those passengers who became seasick.

I'd been told that eating oranges and their *peelings* would prevent seasickness. And, lo and behold, this worked for me! Unfortunately, however, many of the others aboard couldn't seem to quell their nausea; and Willard and I quickly learned that, when we were up on deck, we should stay upwind of the many seasick people throwing up over the sides! The wind sprayed vomit on anyone who was foolish enough to stand toward the rear of the ship.

I don't know if it had anything to do with the weather, but we were told that one of the boilers had blown. Thus, our voyage took an extra day or two.

Finally, however, the weather cleared and, on the eighth day, the Statue of Liberty in New York Harbor came into view. It was a wonderful sight – and not just because of our difficult crossing. That statue is a powerful symbol of promise and welcome, and everyone aboard was moved by it.

★ ★ ★

The trip had given me as much sea-travel as I ever wanted to experience. In addition to feeling cooped up, I feared the water and the creatures who lived in it. We had spotted whales, sharks, and porpoises during the voyage. But even the beautiful sight of porpoises leaping in the luminescent wake of the moonlit ocean wasn't enough to make me want to go to sea again.

So I was quite eager to get off the ship. However, three hours passed after we reached port, before we were allowed to go ashore. As we stood by the rails, we saw many buses lining up on the roads by the pier to take us all to Camp Kilmer in New Jersey. And no sooner did we arrive at the camp, than Willard and I were separated again!

As soon as we stepped off the bus, the wives were sent to the right and the husbands to the left. We women were again confined to our own quarters – in this case, barracks. But, fortunately for me, I was given the same roommate as I'd had on the ship. Like me, she was Slovakian-born, and her name was Matilda.

We were told to put our belongings in our rooms, then line up immediately to walk over to the mess hall for dinner. We stood in line for half an hour before we even got into the mess hall and received our food; so, if we weren't hungry before, we certainly were by the time we were finally fed!

It was immediately clear to us that the Army wasn't going to roll out the red carpet for us. Indeed, almost all of us were very disappointed at the treatment we received. We were told, both outright and in other, subtler ways: "Take what you get. You're only war brides, after all."

But it wasn't easy for me to keep quiet. I'd spent too many years with Aunt Rosa for that. I somehow managed to hold my tongue on that first day in the States, however.

After dinner we were again lined up and marched right back to our barracks. It was about a ten-minute walk, and it made us feel like prisoners. I hadn't expected a parade in my honor for the work I'd done for the Allieds in Germany, but I certainly hadn't expected to be treated like a POW either!

The conditions in the barracks only served to make us feel more like prisoners. The floor boards were about half an inch apart and we could see the mice running back and forth beneath. Thus we kept the light on all through that first night and we got very little sleep. Indeed, we were actually relieved when the base whistle blew at 5:00 a.m. to wake us – since most of us hadn't fallen asleep in the first place. We got out of bed and lined up again to march off to the mess hall for our 6:00 breakfast… It was always the same: wait in line, eat, march back to the barracks.

Later that morning, we were again lined up, this time to go to the dispensary for shots. That was a real disaster because some of the women were pregnant, and they were passing out as they were being immunized. We were standing outside in two long lines on a very warm day. When I got close enough to see the men giving the injections, I recognized one as a GI who used to sell movie tickets at the theater where Aunt Rosa, Willard and I used to go in Degerndorf. That bothered me, because collecting money for tickets hardly seemed adequate training for giving injections and I really doubted that he'd had any medical experience.

I was about six people in line from him, when a woman he was giving a shot to fell to the ground, and something inside me snapped! It was clear to me that this man didn't know what he was doing. His injections were causing so much pain that the pregnant women were simply unable to bear it, and they were passing out.

I stepped out of the line and stomped up to him. "Don't you touch another one of us until I see the officer in charge," I demanded.

He was surprised to hear me speaking English. "Who are you?" he asked.

I didn't answer him; I just repeated, "Get the officer in charge!" Then I turned to the ladies in line and told them in German to yell, "We want to see the officer in charge!"

It took awhile, but eventually a captain, who was the head of the operation, arrived, and he got two new men to administer the shots.

The captain and I had quite a talk, and he stayed and watched as the new men began giving the injections once more. A couple of times, I had to tell the new men where to put the needle and how to do it. My first-aid training at school and during the war had given me this know-how.

Then the captain apologized, explaining that he simply didn't have enough people to do the job.

By that time it was nearly 11:00 a.m., and we were trooped back to the mess hall for lunch. After that, we had the afternoon free, so many of us walked around the barracks, hoping to see our husbands. Unfortunately, we were out of luck.

★   ★   ★

Finally, on our third day in camp, Willard let me know that he would pick me up at 4:00 p.m. to go to town for dinner.

I told him, "You'd better pick me up *and get me out of here,* because I'm ready to swim the Atlantic Ocean back to Germany!"

We took the bus from camp, and, as we got off in New Brunswick, New Jersey, I saw children dressed in weird costumes and masks. Some of them had toy guns that they pointed at us, and they yelled, "Tricks or treats!"

It was my introduction to Halloween, and, given how disgusted I already was with my accommodations in this new country, it certainly wasn't a very pleasant one! After having had guns pointed at me by Americans in Germany, I found it very alarming to have it happen again.

Willard had his arm around me, and as we tried to get away from the trick-or-treaters, he explained Halloween to me, because we'd never celebrated it in Slovakia or Germany.

Then, out of the blue, a man came up to us and

said, "Come with me. My restaurant is right here."

I guess he realized that I was still a bit shaken. What was more, he seemed accustomed to seeing GIs returning to the States with their war brides, so he made a point of helping them to feel at home.

He certainly did so for me, in any case. He served us a good dinner, with a bottle of wine, and said simply, "My treat. Welcome to America." Now, *this* was the America that I soon came to know and love.

The delicious meal and the hospitality did wonders to help me relax after those three days in the barracks. And there was more good news: Willard told me that he had gotten a long leave, and he was taking me home to Minnesota the following day. And that seemed to me a great alternative to having to swim the Atlantic back to Germany!

★ ★ ★

The train ride back to Mankato, Minnesota was long, but beautiful. Willard's dad and his aunt picked us up at the station, then drove us to Nicollet, where Willard and I had a chance to visit many of his other relatives and friends.

At first, Willard's relations were in shock and so was I. This was understandable, I suppose, given that Willard had left for the Army as a teenager, and now he'd returned, not only quite a bit older, but with a foreign-born wife.

Some of my shock, on the other hand, was simply a result of being so exhausted from all of the traveling we'd done. But, the next morning, after everyone had gotten a good night's sleep, the shock wore off and all of us got along just fine.

★ ★ ★

In mid-December, Willard left for a new Army assignment in Chicago. I was to follow him the first week in January. It was not easy for me to stay behind with his relatives, because everything was so different from what I'd been accustomed to in Germany.

Munich was a huge, bustling city. And even St. Margarethen, though in the country, was only a short train ride from the city. The farm land of southern Minnesota, however, was an entirely different story. For one thing, it was much more isolated; and there was really nothing to see or do in the little town of Nicollet, Minnesota. When I didn't hear from Willard for nearly a week after his departure to Illinois, I just couldn't help weeping. But, finally, he telephoned and told me to come and join him.

He'd found an efficiency apartment in a hotel on 53rd and Cornell South, which was just a ten-minute walk to the 5th Army Headquarters where he worked. There, we met a very nice Jewish lady named Mrs. Segansky, who worked at the hotel desk, where we paid our weekly rent.

Mrs. Segansky asked us lots of questions. And, when she learned that I was a war bride, she became very interested in us and asked if I would like to work at the hotel desk, as well. Since I was now pregnant and Willard was working some night shifts, the desk was the perfect place for me. I didn't even have to leave the building to go to work.

★ ★ ★

Our daughter, Margaret, who was named for the town of St. Margarethen, was born in April of 1949; and Mrs. Segansky let me keep her in the office with me for about two months. Then Willard wheeled her in the buggy every morning to the 5th Army Headquarters and placed her in the day-care center there. Since Willard's Army check was small and my dependent check had been reduced, as a government cost-cutting measure, we were having a hard time making it financially.

Thus, Willard decided to get out of the Army and go to school to acquire additional job training. We left Chicago in January of 1950 and returned to Mankato, Minnesota, where Willard received his high-school diploma. In March, we moved to Minneapolis, so Willard could attend the Minneapolis School of Business. He and I both worked part-time, while he went to school.

★ ★ ★

After a couple of years, Willard graduated and got a full-time job with Dakota Transfer – the same company he'd been working part-time for. In July of 1953, we purchased our first home in Bloomington, Minnesota. It was still a struggle financially, so we both worked all sorts of full-time and part-time jobs. These included everything from pumping gas to sales jobs to positions with the streetcar company.

★ ★ ★

In December of 1955, our son was born. We named him Wendell, in honor of Wendelstein Mountain, which stood behind St. Margarethen. I returned to work at the G.E.M. Store, just a couple of months after his birth.

★ ★ ★

On January 22, 1956, I received two letters containing bad news. The first was from Czechoslovakia. One of my brothers had written to inform me that my mother had just died, at the age of 59. The second letter was from Aunt Rosa, who wrote to let us know that Uncle Georg had passed away the preceding February. He had died while cutting down a pine tree.

The reason why my aunt had waited so long to tell us this was that she knew how fond Uncle Georg and I were of each other, and that made it all the more difficult for her to convey the news. She went on to say that she had been alone for ten months and that she needed me to come home to Germany.

I just didn't have the heart to tell her that we didn't have enough money at that point for the trip. So, Willard and I went to the bank and made arrangements for Margaret and me to go visit Aunt Rosa after school got out in June. We sent Wendell to stay with Willard's cousin, Louise in Mankato. Every weekend Willard went down to visit him there. Although these arrangements worked out fine, it ended up to be a very long six weeks for all of us – being split up as we were.

During my visit to Germany, Aunt Rosa confessed that Uncle Georg had been ashamed to tell people that Willard and I lived in a house similar to a chicken coop in the U.S.! It took me a minute to realize what she meant. In one of my letters to my aunt and uncle, I had described our house in Bloomington, Minnesota as being made of wood. Yet, in Bavaria, wood-frame structures were unheard-of as human dwellings. Homes and offices were built of brick, stone, or cement, and wooden buildings were considered suitable only for animals!

★ ★ ★

In the years that followed, Willard and I were both very active at Mt. Calvary Lutheran Church and School in Richfield, Minnesota. We were able to send both of our children to school there, for kindergarten through the sixth grade.

In 1959, we planned our first family vacation. We hoped to spend a week in the Black Hills of South Dakota – provided, of course, that the sixty dollars we'd set aside for the trip would last for seven days. To make sure it did, we ate a lot of sandwiches, charged the gasoline for the trip and slept two nights in a tent we'd borrowed. We also spent a couple more nights in the car and only one night at a motel.

It wasn't very glamorous, Heaven knows; but we all had lots of fun for those sixty dollars. And we enjoyed the Black Hills so much that we returned there again for another visit in 1964.

★ ★ ★

In 1961, Margaret finished the sixth grade and went to Portland Jr. High School in Bloomington. Wendell, meanwhile, started first grade at Mt. Calvary.

★ ★ ★

In July of 1965, we traveled west to Yellowstone National Park. We also saw the Passion Play in Spearfish, South Dakota, and, of course, the Corn Palace at Mitchell.

The following month, the entire family went to Germany for three weeks. When we arrived, Aunt Rosa informed us that my father had died earlier that year in Czechoslovakia at the age of 72.

While we were in St. Margarethen, we all helped my aunt with the villa's upkeep and yard work. But we also found plenty of time to climb the mountains and, of course, to visit and talk about old times.

I think that Aunt Rosa may have carried a lot of guilt into her older years about how she'd treated me during the war. She knew that she was very tough on me. Not physically, but in the things she'd demanded of me. But I held no resentment about her behavior. I realized that, without her strict and exacting ways, I might have made a mistake in my work and been jailed or killed. And I know for sure that she never asked me to take a risk that she herself would not have taken.

★ ★ ★

We returned to Minnesota after our stay in Germany; and, two years later, in December of 1967, I was again able to visit with one of my family members from Europe. The phone rang one day and I simply couldn't believe who I heard on the other end. It was my brother, Štefo calling from *Detroit, Michigan!* Because I had only received a couple of letters a year from my sister, Rosa and she had not mentioned anything about Štefo taking a trip, it was a great surprise to learn that he was in the United States.

Štefo was now an engineer at a manufacturing plant in Czechoslovakia. He told me that he had received a permit to stay in the U.S. for eight weeks, so that he could learn everything possible about the automotive plants here. The Russians wanted him to learn all about them and bring the information home.

But his permit from the Czech government explicitly stated that he was not to leave Detroit. So he wanted me to travel there to see him. I talked with him for quite a while on the phone, and I spoke with the family he was staying with, who were of Slovak descent. I explained to Štefo that it was not practical for us to go to Michigan because of our jobs. Instead, we sent a round-trip ticket on Northwest Airlines, so he could fly to Minnesota and visit us. We were careful to send the ticket in his host-family's name, so the Russian government would have no way of knowing that he'd left Detroit.

When the family picked up the ticket at the Detroit airport and walked to the designated concourse, the father gave the ticket to Štefo, who then boarded the plane. This stealthy procedure reminded me of some of my operations back in Munich during the war.

As we waited at the gate where Štefo's flight was arriving at the Minneapolis/St. Paul International Airport, Willard asked me, "How are we going to recognize him?"

Because I had not seen him since 1943 – nearly 25 years – I had to admit that I was not sure I *would* recognize him.

But, as we watched the people coming out of the airplane, I suddenly exclaimed, "There he is."

"Are you sure?" Willard asked.

I was fairly sure, but, in the end, it was Štefo who made the first decisive move. He instantly recognized me from a recent photograph he had with him.

He didn't have any luggage, so we went straight to the car. He asked to sit in the back seat. This seemed an odd request, but he said that he wanted to be able to look out the back to see if anyone was following us.

When we finally turned into our driveway he said, "Let me run into the house, so no one will see me."

He was somehow convinced that a vehicle was following us. And no sooner had Willard stopped the car, than Štefo dashed out and ran into the house.

All that Saturday morning, he stayed indoors, and, every thirty minutes or so, he would get up and peek through the living-room curtains. He claimed that he'd seen the same car drive by our house several times.

Willard and I started to think he was just imagining things, that he simply wasn't accustomed to being in a country where people were free to come and go as they pleased.

We, therefore, managed to talk Štefo into going out that evening, so he could meet some of our friends at the V.F.W. club. But, around 10:00 p.m., he said, "We've been here for two hours, had a couple of drinks, and danced a lot. It's been great. But now we'd better go back to your house."

It was clear that he was still afraid that he was being followed or that someone would spot him out in public. And, all the way home, he watched every car – obviously believing that someone was after him.

But we finally did understand his concern, when, the next morning, Willard and I both saw the same car drive down our street several times. Each time, its occupants looked intently at our house.

Later that afternoon, as we drove Štefo back to the airport for his return to Detroit, he said, "Look behind you."

Sure enough, it was the same car that had

repeatedly driven past our house that morning and, what was more, it followed us all the way to the airport!

We got Štefo on the plane, and his hosts picked him up in Detroit. The next morning we received a call from that family. They said, "Everything's okay. Štefo is at work."

They also told us just how big a risk Štefo had taken in coming to visit us. Štefo's family in Czechoslovakia had been told by the Russians that, if Štefo hadn't returned to Czechoslovakia by midnight on the 31st of December, they would all be shot! At last, we finally understood why Štefo had told us he was leaving the U.S. a day early to make certain he got back home on time.

★ ★ ★

In May of the following year, Willard's dad died at the age of 73. And, two months later, we all went to Germany again. Aunt Rosa told us that she wanted to adopt me as her legal daughter. She told Willard that she needed his permission to do this, since my father wouldn't give it to her before he'd died.

Willard and I both agreed to it and we all felt that my last name shouldn't change as a result. The German judge who handled the matter was nice, but tough. He made very sure that Willard understood the papers he was signing. We then spent two weeks with Aunt Rosa, who was now my mother, at the villa in St. Margarethen. I had no trouble calling her Mother instead of Aunt, and our kids called her *grossmütter* – grandmother – which she liked very much.

We also spent another two weeks traveling

Rosa Schneider in 1968

with our children through Germany, Austria, and Switzerland. I had been working at Control Data Corporation for several years, performing quality control inspections on their powerful scientific computers, and I had received a letter from William Norris, the president of Control Data to the officials at the CERN atomic laboratories in Bern, Switzerland. The letter allowed me to enter the facility and see several of the computers, which I had helped build, in actual operation. It was a great thrill to see my inspection stamp right there on the equipment, and the people at CERN were very gracious hosts.

We also traveled through Liechtenstein and finally to Luxembourg, where we boarded the plane to return to the U.S.

That fall, Margaret started as a freshman at St. Olaf College, and Wendell entered the eighth grade at Portland Jr. High in Bloomington, Minnesota.

★ ★ ★

Then, a year later, in 1969, we were again called to Germany. Mother had fallen ill, and I had no choice but to go to her aid. I made the trip alone and stayed for two weeks. It was difficult to find the time amidst my work schedule; but, because I was now her daughter and she was quite sick, the German government considered it my legal responsibility to see that she was properly cared for.

I spent time with her and made the necessary arrangements to ensure that she would be well looked after, once I returned to the States. By the time I left, she was feeling better. But I knew that she was not getting any younger and that this would not be the last time she would need my care. There would, eventually, be some very difficult decisions for me to make – ones which would affect Willard and our kids.

CHAPTER ELEVEN

RETURN TO EUROPE AND HOME TO THE U.S.A.

January of 1971 was bitterly cold in Minnesota. That month, Willard and I received a letter from the Mayor of St. Margarethen. He wrote that my mother's health was failing and that it was my legal duty to come back to Germany and take care of her. We also received a letter from my mother Rosa that said she wanted our whole family to come and live with her in the Villa Waldeck. She said that, if we didn't come to live with her, the German government would put her in a nursing home. Then they would sell all her belongings to pay for her stay there.

"Once they do that," she wrote, "you and Willard won't be able to say or do anything about the house, its contents, or me. The government will take over."

Picking up our family and moving to Europe, after over 20 years in the Twin Cities, was a very difficult decision for Willard and me. We both had good jobs. Our daughter Margaret would soon be graduating from St. Olaf College in Northfield, Minnesota.

And Wendell was a junior at Kennedy High School and involved in many school activities. It was going to be very hard to ask him to give up all of that so that he could go live in a foreign country.

For months our family discussions on the matter went back and forth.

"We'll go," we'd decide one day.

Then, the next, it was, "No. It's just too much to ask. Too much trouble and expense for everyone."

But we knew that we couldn't leave Rosa in such a helpless situation, so on the debate went. And the only thing we were sure of was that a final decision on the subject absolutely had to be made by May.

When, at last, we reached one, I wrote my mother to tell her that we were coming to live with her in Germany. For the next three months, the whole family was busy. There was something momentous to do every week. We had to quit jobs, sell furniture, and have garage sales. And, in the midst of all the moving preparations, we had to make another move. Margaret had been hired for a position as a German language teacher at Adlai Stevenson High School in Prairie View, Illinois. And, even as we prepared to move ourselves, we had to help her move to Buffalo Grove, Illinois – which was about ten miles from Prairie View.

★ ★ ★

The move to Germany was particularly difficult for Wendell. It was hard for him to leave his friends and classmates behind, when he only had two more years to go before graduation. And, of course, when the actual day of our departure rolled around, he was a very unhappy young man. Nevertheless, in early September of 1971, Willard, Wendell, Wendell's dog,

Regi, and I flew out of Minneapolis/St. Paul International Airport and headed for Munich.

Our friend, Hans met us at the airport to pick us up and drive us to St. Margarethen. We soon located all of our luggage and belongings except for one: Regi, Wendell's beautiful Norwegian elkhound. As if the decision to move hadn't been tough enough for Wendell, now the airlines had lost his dog!

It was a very poor start to our life overseas. But, after making some frantic inquiries, we discovered that the baggage handlers in Frankfurt had accidentally put Regi on a plane heading to Chicago, instead of Munich. And, two days later, we collected poor Regi at the Munich airport.

She seemed as happy to see us as we were to see her. The airline workers brought her to us – leading her on a leash, as if she was a show dog. They assured us that she had received very good care because she was such a good and beautiful dog.

I've often thought since that it was a shame they didn't have frequent-flyer miles back then – especially for dogs. Regi would definitely have racked up a free ticket, after all those trips across the Atlantic!

When we returned to the villa with our pet, Mother greeted her as though she'd known her for years. And it was clear that Regi liked Rosa, too.

★ ★ ★

We registered Wendell in the Munich American High School, and he began his classes in October. At Christmas time, Margaret came to Germany for two weeks during her school break. Wendell told her how small the classes were at school and that it meant he could be in whatever sports he wanted. As a result, we attended many of Wendell's games in football, basketball, track, and soccer. This often meant traveling to different American armed forces bases in Germany, Italy, Spain, and England. But it was an interesting way to see the rest of Europe.

★ ★ ★

My mother's health continued to decline, and on February 9, 1972, she passed away. In her last days she didn't speak about the war or her life, but only about the peace that she expected to find in Heaven. We had her cremated and her ashes were buried in the same cemetery in which her two husbands had been laid to rest.

★ ★ ★

In June, 1972, Willard and Wendell went to the States for two weeks to check on our properties in Bloomington and Sauk Centre. Wendell was still not too happy in Germany, and he wanted to see his old friends back in Bloomington. In fact, he missed home so much that, as he said good-bye to me before leaving Munich, he also said, "I won't come back with Dad."

I was so taken aback by his remark, that all I could say was, "Really?" But, inside, I was very concerned about what he'd do.

After a week in Minnesota, Willard called and told me not to worry about Wendell staying in the States.

"He's finding out how great he's got it in Germany," Willard explained. "Some of his friends didn't make any sports teams, because there were so many boys going out for each one."

Willard also explained that Wendell was able to

tell his friends about the teams he was on, all the traveling he was doing, and how many trophies his school's teams had won.

★ ★ ★

When the two of them returned to Germany, Regi and I picked them up at the Munich airport. Willard knew the exact location in the terminal where I was waiting for them, because we had a little trick in mind for Wendell. When Wendell got off the plane he was surprised to see that I was not there.

He asked Willard, "Where's Mom?"

And Willard replied, "You told Mother that you were not coming back, so there was no reason for her to drive to Munich, because I could take the train home on my own."

At this, Wendell stopped and put down his suitcase; and I could see the tears in his eyes, even from where Regi and I were hiding behind a big pillar. But Regi quickly spotted Wendell, and she began to whimper and yip.

I let her go, and she dashed to Wendell, before he could even pick up his suitcase.

What a joy it was to see them both so happy! I got a big hug from both of my men, and Regi got a big hug from Wendell. We all got in the car, talking non-stop about everything which had happened over the preceding two weeks.

Wendell was also very excited about the prospect of seeing the Olympics in Munich that summer, and he told us that he had shared those hopes with his friends. When the time came, and people from all over the world began to pour into Munich, we had visitors from Bloomington and Sioux Falls,

South Dakota. And we all went to the Olympics and had a great time.

Unfortunately, the Munich games were scarred by the terrorist massacre of the Israeli athletes. Our guests had left the Olympic grounds with us just half an hour before the terrorists attacked. So, we ended up seeing the tragedy unfold on television, along with the rest of the world.

★ ★ ★

Wendell eagerly awaited the start of school in the fall of 1972. It was also about that time that the Army Security Agency in Bad Aibling asked Willard to come to work for them. They really needed someone with his experience and his excellent command of German. It was a good fit for us, because it cut the cost of Wendell's tuition and it meant that we could shop at the PX and the commissary in Bad Aibling. Not only were prices cheaper on the base, but there were many items available there, such as bleach and good cuts of meat, which we couldn't get on the German market.

I was invited to the Ladies Auxiliary Club, and I was given a membership card by the President, who was the Colonel's wife. I was asked to speak at the next meeting on German customs and how to go shopping in the local stores. It was not easy for some of the ladies to refrain from touching merchandise, yet this behavior was very much frowned upon in Germany. Instead, customers looked at or pointed to the stores' goods, telling the sales clerks what they wanted to see. The clerks then brought out the goods for closer inspection. As if to underscore this, there were no self-serve stores, like we have here in the States.

German ladies also dressed nicely and tastefully,

when they went shopping. Going to stores in hair curlers, bare feet, or very casual clothes was considered a big breach of social etiquette. And, of course, doing any of these things made American women stick out like a sore thumb amidst the Germans. Nevertheless, the Americans always seemed surprised when they realized that the locals were staring at them for these blunders.

When I tried to explain such cultural differences, a few of the American ladies said to me, "The Germans better accept us the way we are, because we won the war, so we should be able to do things our way."

I, in turn, had to go into my explanation – and it always ended up being a long one. "Yes, our men won the war, but that was nearly 27 years ago. It's 1972 now and we are *guests* in Germany. When I first came to Munich as a foreigner in 1939, I, too, had to learn to dress and act differently."

Of course, I didn't tell them how glad and grateful I was then for the opportunity to wear nice clothes and be well-groomed!

★ ★ ★

There were many parties planned at the club on the Bad Aibling base. To help the U.S. and German forces coexist more happily, they started to invite German military men and their wives to these get-togethers. After a couple of parties at our base, the Germans returned the favor by inviting us to the German base Degerndorf, where their alpine army troops were stationed. About twenty American couples went, and we had a wonderful time.

But the biggest party we all attended was when

the Germans had their *fasching*, which is similar to the Mardi Gras in the U.S. We planned a big American-style picnic on our base in June of 1974, and roughly 2,000 people – both Germans and Americans – came. The Germans really enjoyed our hot dogs, potato chips, and pop. But the biggest benefit was that both nationalities got to know and understand each other better.

That was very rewarding for both Willard and me, and it represented a real step forward in improving relations between our two countries. The German newspaper in Bad Aibling covered the event. They wrote about what a great time everyone had, how nice it was to be invited, and what good friends the Americans were proving to be.

Our daughter, Margaret and her roommate, Janet, who was also a teacher, came for the summer break to visit us. Wendell had graduated in June from the Munich high school, and, in September, he left to attend St. Cloud State College back in Minnesota. So, September of 1973 found Willard, Regi, and me living in the Villa Waldeck and busy promoting goodwill between the Germans and Americans.

★ ★ ★

In April of that same year, my brother, Štefo, and my sister, Mila, surprised us by coming to visit us for three days. They had gotten a special visa from the Czechoslovak government to do so. The previous August, before Margaret and Wendell had returned to the U.S., we'd all planned to go to Czechoslovakia for a brief visit. Unfortunately, however, it was not to be.

Willard was working at the base club until 3:00 a.m. Saturday morning, so the kids and I went to pick him up for the drive to Vienna, where we had a hotel reservation. After getting to our hotel room around 7:00 a.m. Saturday, we doubled-checked our passports. Our whole family each carried two U.S. passports: a maroon military passport, and the standard olive green civilian passport. Using the green passports, we got our visas to go to Czechoslovakia at the Czech embassy. By 9:00 a.m., the papers were filled out for the four of us, our photos were taken, and we had paid the fee in schillings. At 10:00 a.m., Willard and the kids received their passports from the Czech attaché, but my passport was not with the others.

Willard asked the official, "Where is my wife's passport?"

"You and the kids may go, but she can't," the man replied.

Willard explained that the reason why we were going to Czechoslovakia was because it was *my* birthplace. And, at 11:30 a.m., we finally got my passport back, but the Czech government refused to give me a visa. So we all went back to the hotel to call my brother, who was waiting for us at the Czech border, and tell him that we would not be coming. It was a great disappointment for both families. We did, however, spend the rest of the weekend in Vienna and we managed to have some fun there.

When Willard returned to work at the base the following Monday, the security officers told him, "It was a good thing you didn't cross into Czechoslovakia, because we would have sent you packing for the U.S., the moment you came back across the border into Austria!"

We had no idea how they knew that we'd tried

to go to Czechoslovakia. None of us had said a word to anyone about the trip, and we were over 400 kilometers away when we'd tried to obtain the necessary visas.

But perhaps the German security officers had learned that we'd gone to the Czech Embassy. Maybe we'd even been followed after leaving the base? To this day, we aren't sure how they found out about it.

★ ★ ★

Later that year, Margaret and Wendell returned to the Villa Waldeck to spend Christmas vacation with us, and we told them that we hoped to sell the house and go back to Minnesota in July. When all of our German and American friends in the area found out that we were planning to return to the U.S., they were very sad. But we promised them all that we would be in Germany long enough to help host the big picnic in June, which had been on the drawing board for over a year.

We put the Villa Waldeck up for sale in the spring of 1974. Lots of our American friends bought furnishings, pictures, ceramics, crystal, and many of our other things so that the moving process was simpler for us. Our German friends also helped us by spreading the news about the sale.

In May, my sister, Mila and my brother, Štefo and his wife came from Czechoslovakia to spend a weekend with us. It was great to see them! I had worried that, since their government would not let me in to visit them, we would never get the chance to see each other again.

The Villa Waldeck was sold soon thereafter to a Professor Schultz; but Willard and I weren't required to move out until the end of June, 1974. It was then that I realized just how many memories were in that house. Not only for me and Willard, but for our children, as well. I had, blessedly, been able to share the surrounding roads, the forests, and the mountains with my family, and I was deeply grateful for this.

But we couldn't leave without throwing the promised picnic for all of our German and American friends; and it was, happily, a huge success! An airplane flew overhead, dropping five precision parachutists. How beautiful it was to watch them drift down to a nearby landing! Everyone was watching them, faces turned up to the sky, and smiling.

Seeing the Germans and Americans happy together like this meant a lot to us. We hoped that we had truly helped to improve relations between them, and they offered us many kind words at the picnic which confirmed this for us. We were sad to say good-bye to it all, but Willard and I knew that our real home was in the U.S.A. with our children.

★ ★ ★

On June 18, 1974, a 40-foot trailer arrived to move our belongings. Even with all the help we had, it still took us two days to load the trailer. We had carefully selected those pieces that meant the most to us, and we'd sold the rest to our neighbors and friends. What we kept, however, is still with us to this day, in our house in Minnesota – lovely and cherished reminders of Rosa, the Villa Waldeck, and our lives in Germany.

Then Willard, Regi, and I left the villa and began the journey home on June 20th; and, six weeks later, the 40-foot trailer arrived in the U.S. as well.

During the three years we lived in Germany, 22 friends from the U.S. visited us for periods ranging from two to four weeks. Many stayed with us at the villa, and we were able to take them to the local places of interest, as well as driving them to such nearby countries as Austria, Italy, Liechtenstein, Switzerland, and France.

But, as much as they enjoyed visiting us, it was clear when we got back to the States, that these friends were even happier to have us home once more. When the 40-foot trailer arrived, we had plenty of help getting the furnishings into the house and seeing that we were settled.

The next day we had a homecoming party. Our barrel of German beer and champagne made the journey across "the big pond" in excellent condition, although it was a close shave for the beer, which had no preservatives in it! With little advance notice, about 40 friends still were able to come over to our house and have a glass of German beer or champagne with us in order to welcome us back.

That summer was a busy one, with lots of yard work to do and the task of fixing up our lake place at Sauk Centre. Fortunately, we had a lot of help. At the end of August, Margaret went back to Illinois, where she was teaching, and Wendell returned to St. Cloud State University.

★ ★ ★

At Christmas time, we had a wonderful surprise: Margaret announced that she was planning to be married on July 26, 1975. Walter Plank, of Morton Grove, Illinois, was to be our new son-in-law. And, when the big day finally arrived, we were blessed with a wonderful wedding and beautiful, warm weather.

★ ★ ★

In November, 1977, Willard and I moved from Bloomington to a new and bigger house in Eden Prairie, Minnesota. And, that Christmas, Wendell told us that he would be getting married on May 27, 1978. So, Christmas was certainly our time of year for wedding announcements!

But, before Wendell's wedding took place, our first grandchild, Gregory John Plank, was born on March 27th, which is also my birthday. It's our son-in-law Walter's date of birth, as well. So, March 27th is very popular for new arrivals to our family!

★ ★ ★

Our son Wendell was married to Paula Uphoff on May 27, 1978. And our second grandchild, Susanne Marie Plank, was born on October 13, 1981.

The following year, our third grandchild, April Maria Daluge, was born on September 14, 1982. And, her brother, Jonathan Edwin Daluge, arrived on March 30, 1988, missing his cousin's, uncle's, and grandmother's birthdays by only three days!

★ ★ ★

In the spring of 1990, following the fall of the Iron Curtain, I received the good news that I no longer needed a special visa or special protection to go to Czechoslovakia. So, in September of 1990, Willard and I finally made the trip to see my three brothers and two sisters. Although we had seen Štefo and Mila in the early '70s, I had not seen the others for 47 years!

It was a wonderful reunion. Fifteen of my family members got together in a restaurant in Trnava, Czechoslovakia, where my sister Mila lived. We stayed with Štefo and his wife, Marischka in Brestovany, which is only 20 kilometers away from Trnava. We were able to meet all of my nieces and nephews – all 39 of them – as we visited my brother's and sister's homes around Slovakia.

All the people in my home town of Paderovce knew we were coming. Indeed, I saw several of my school friends, but I hardly recognized them. Of course, they knew who I was, because of my American clothes, if nothing else. It took me a couple of days before I was able to regain fluency in Slovak, so that I could interpret in English for Willard.

We were on the go from morning until late evening on every one of our sixteen days in Czechoslovakia. Often we found ourselves eating four or five meals a day as we visited. Willard was good about receiving the hospitality of our hosts. He tried eating almost everything, but we felt bad because they had so little to give. It was amazing to see how Communism had turned a once-thriving nation into such a poverty-stricken land! Nevertheless, in true Slovak style, they rolled out the best red carpet they had for us.

It was hard to leave Czechoslovakia, but, once we were on the plane for home, we both issued sighs of relief. We hadn't realized how hectic our pace had been nor how tired we were. In fact, it took both of us almost a week to recover from our jet lag and get back onto a normal schedule.

In 1992, we returned to Europe again. This time we spent two weeks in Slovakia and two weeks visiting our friends in Germany, Austria, Switzerland, and

Liechtenstein. In Germany, we got to go into the Villa Waldeck, as well as visit with our close friend, the Mayor of St. Margarethen and many others. In Liechtenstein, we arrived to find that we were a few months too late. Our friend, the King of Liechtenstein, had died a few months earlier. He was a very down-to-earth man, who we had met in the early '70s, when Willard was working for Army Security. The King also ran a jewelry store and had sold Willard a couple of watches. Although we had never gotten to know his children, we spoke with them briefly on our visit.

They were very friendly and they told us, "Well, since you knew the folks, you can go on up and take a look at the house," which meant the King's residence in the castle, overlooking the principality.

When we reached Slovakia, we again found that we were a bit too late. My brother, Josef, had died just two weeks earlier! But the division of Czechoslovakia into the Czech Republic and the Slovakian Republic in 1991 seemed to be working out. My family told us that after a year and a half, the Slovaks were doing fine. The children were learning English in the schools, and many American businesses were coming into the country.

We also took the time to tour those parts of Slovakia that are well known for their excellent crystal and pottery. We visited some very beautiful and picturesque old castles, as well – some of which dated back to the days of the Roman Empire.

We enjoyed the four weeks of traveling very much, especially since the pace was not as hectic as during our trip in 1990. Because we were able to visit all of the places we'd known, Willard and I returned to the U.S. feeling that we had finally said good-bye to Europe. And neither of us have felt any desire to return. Instead, we are now hoping to bring my niece and nephews from Slovakia to visit this beautiful country we call home – the United States of America.

CHAPTER TWELVE

LOOKING BACK
SOME CLOSING THOUGHTS FROM WILLARD (BUBY) DALUGE

As Agnes and I look back, we realize that the changes in Europe from 1946 to 1992 were great and surprising. The surprising part was that so much of Europe was so completely devastated by World War II. When I first saw Munich as a young soldier of 19, this city, which Agnes had known so well as a place of beauty and bustling activity, was decimated. Everywhere there were broken and damaged buildings. Many were completely leveled. Huge hills of brick and concrete, the debris of what were once apartment buildings and offices, were piled on every block. Many streets had only a narrow track, one- or two-people wide, that wound in and out of the rubble. And the dust from the cement and mortar was *everywhere*.

The people, however, were already working with hammers and sledges, chipping the mortar off of the bricks so that they could be used again. Slowly but surely, large and neatly arranged stacks of bricks appeared near the streets and alleys. Already, the people of Munich were looking to rebuild their city and their lives.

Packs of ten to twelve kids roamed all over, begging for food or for cigarettes – which they could trade for food. We would often see them hanging around the dumpsters outside our army base, hoping to find something edible in the scraps which the GIs threw out. Even when the weather was hot and the smell from the dumpsters was thick and choking, the kids still found things to eat amongst the rotting food, and eat them they did. They had no choice, since many of them had lost their homes and families to the bombings and the other ravages of six years of war.

Thus, what a contrast it was for us to visit Munich again in 1992! The last time Agnes and I saw the city, we would not have believed that it was the same place we'd known in 1946. By 1992, new buildings, many of them almost exotic in their design and construction, had sprung up from what were blocks and blocks of rubble. Even the airport, which had been heavily bombed, was moved and rebuilt into one of the most modern in the world.

The highways, such as the autobahn, had also been badly damaged by the Allied forces. Especially during the closing months of the war, as the Luftwaffe's air fields were put out of commission by bombings, the Germans used the autobahns for landing strips for their fighters. Even after the war, one could still see the black marks on the autobahn from the wheel marks and engine exhaust of the aircraft. And in the woods and brush along the autobahn, it was not uncommon to see the wreckage of Messerschmitts and other German aircraft. They had crashed there during unsuccessful take-offs or landings, often after damaging duels with American Mustangs or Thunderbolt fighter planes.

Of course, the Allies caught on to the fact that the Germans were using the autobahn for this purpose, so they themselves soon became prime targets for strafing and bombing missions. And the bridge decks and overpasses were blown up so that they were standing on end or tilted at crazy angles.

This sort of destruction necessitated long and tortuous detours, which made every trip around the Munich area a real adventure. I'm sure it was the same throughout Germany and the rest of Europe, for that matter.

The autobahns (and *autostradas* in Italy) have since been rebuilt and improved to handle auto traffic that moves at very high speeds. And new bridges and tunnels (one 26-kilometers long) have been constructed in the Alps to make travel between the countries much easier.

However, in 1946, people in Munich and Bavaria were less concerned with travel than they were with simply surviving. This was especially true during the first winters after the war, which were bitterly cold. Few buildings had any heat. And the American troops were little better off. We always said that a person wasn't really cold until the numbness had worked its way into his knees. We often saw groups of people and families huddled around makeshift fires in the rubble, trying to keep warm. And, nearly fifty years later, I can still fully recall the bone-chilling cold of those winters.

But, even with all of the changes, there are still

many reminders of the war to be seen in Germany today. After the war, it was divided into zones controlled by each of the Allied powers. The American zone in particular was cleaned up quite thoroughly and was also rebuilt to a greater degree than the French, British, or Soviet zones. In these other zones, one can still see the remains of pill boxes, as well as bullet and shell holes on the buildings which survived the bombing. And, of course, the concentration and death camps have been preserved as reminders of the Holocaust. There are also some signs of the displaced-persons (DP) camps that housed tens of thousands of refugees – Holocaust survivors, and others who had lost their homes and families. Though the camps were crowded and confining, many people felt they were better off in them, being fed by the Americans, than wandering around in Germany. The DPs knew that their fellow countrymen were so busy trying to survive themselves that they could offer very little assistance to those who were less fortunate.

In general, however, the war isn't mentioned much in German schools. This is as it should be, since most of the war deserves to be put behind us.

After the war, transportation was very basic. The train stations were badly damaged. For example, before the war, the Bahnhof in Munich had large glass canopies that protected the loading platforms for the trains. All of this glass was blown out by the bombing. There was also a huge hole in the ceiling of the terminal building that was not repaired until 1948.

The trains themselves were in little better shape. They consisted largely of a few engines connected to a few cars, which were certainly the worse for having been through the war. The cars were unheated and many of their windows had been broken or blown out. And, with so many holes from bullets and shell fragments, train travel in Germany became "air conditioned" year round!

Today's German trains are very comfortable and are used by most working people to get to and from their jobs. Thus, the trains run on very precise and frequent schedules.

The famed Orient Express, which managed to escape damage during the war, has somehow retained its air of elegance. The red velvet upholstery and curtains were still in place when we rode it. Agnes and I marveled at the suspension system in the passenger and dining cars. Even the sharpest of turns hardly produced a ripple in a cup of coffee. It was one of the smoothest and quietest rides we've ever experienced.

For American troops, the main sources of transportation were authorized truck transport or our thumbs (unauthorized hitchhiking). What automobiles we saw after the war did not run on gasoline or petroleum products, which were very scarce. Instead, they were powered by coke (coal) burners, which heated water to generate steam. These cars could not travel very fast and they put out a lot of exhaust. What a contrast to the cars of today, zooming at speeds well over a hundred miles an hour on the modern autobahns!

The people of Bavaria and Munich set themselves to the task of rebuilding, almost as soon as the surrender was signed. And they didn't stop until the task was done. The Alps and the beautiful countryside around Munich remains the same as it has been for hundreds of years. The wars and progress of humankind seem to have had little effect on these great works of nature. And, although all of the modern conveniences and sources of power are available to them today, many Bavarians continue to heat their homes with wood and coal.

Their sense of hospitality and good cheer has changed little, as well. Each time we returned to Germany, in the '70s and the '90s, we were greeted with as much familiarity and warmth as if they had just seen us yesterday! I remember arriving on a return visit in the 1970's at the Bad Aibling fire station, after spending decades in the U.S., and hearing a voice shouting across the road, "Herr Daluge! Herr Daluge!" Being remembered like that is the best kind of welcome in the world!

No one epitomized the steady, unchanging traits of the people of Bavaria more than Rosa Schnieder. Agnes's aunt, who later adopted her as a daughter, was strong-willed and self-directed, traits she'd carried since her girlhood. There was Rosa's way and then there was the *wrong* way. And woe be to anyone who was unable to recognize the difference!

Which is not to say that she was arbitrary or irrational. She would listen carefully and weigh the pros and cons of a question. But, once she had made up her mind, that was it. And this was as true of her in the 1970s as it was during the war. Even after losing her second husband in the mid-1950s and living alone in the Villa Waldeck for over twenty years, she still possessed the same commanding presence and air of authority.

She was insistent on her ability to take care of

herself. So much so that she wouldn't even let the Mayor of St. Margarethen, who lived next door to her, help her with the maintenance work. She would only accept help with replacing tiles on the roof and with sweeping the chimney. Our family always pitched in to help her whenever any of us were visiting, especially with the heavier outside work and the indoor cleaning and maintenance. Nevertheless, Rosa was able to continue to split her own firewood right up to the time she went into the hospital. And her strength was so great that she could out split any of us younger folk.

After the war, Rosa was excited to talk about her secret work against Hitler. Her intense hatred of the German dictator never lessened. She also talked about the attitude shared by many of her generation, who had survived two world wars, but lost everything they owned. This had first occurred during the Weimar period after World War I, and then again during World War II. It was an attitude summed up in this little ditty they used to sing:

Is und trink
Solang dir's schmeckt
Schon Zweimal ist uns
S'geld verreckt

(Eat and drink
As long as it tastes
Because two times has our
Money gone bad)

When we returned to Europe in 1992, we made a point of visiting all the people, countries, and places that we'd known during our previous stays. As we did, we realized that many of them had passed away, and the ones who were still alive were now showing the effects of the war and the hard life that they'd had to endure then and in the years immediately following V-E Day.

As in Munich and Bavaria, the places we saw had changed little, except for the new buildings that replaced the ones damaged or destroyed in the war. After our many previous visits, this last trip made Agnes and I realize that these places no longer had the appeal for us they once did. And, since we have retired, the cost of travel and accommodations is no longer as affordable for us as it once was.

All in all, the war years and the post-war period made us accept what came. We learned to make the most of what we had, because we never had anyone else to help us. We tried to instill these attitudes in our children, and it seems to have taken. Our daughter, Margaret, teaches five different high-school German classes each day. She has developed many programs for the school's language department.

Our son, Wendell, is a major in the U.S. Army and has many medals for his accomplishments during a distinguished career.

Having never been in Slovakia before the Iron Curtain came down, my only images and ideas of what life was like there came from what Agnes had told me. These visits to places, where the history that I had only read about was actually made, were very exciting for me. Bratislava and its castle, for example, were absolutely fascinating. In this castle, Maria Theresa mothered many of the men and women, who became the heads of European royal families. In addition to items that belonged to her and her period, there are also relics that date back to Roman times. The "Blue Danube," which is actually quite muddy at that point, flows through Bratislava on its way to Budapest.

By following the Small Carpathian Mountains north through the region where Agnes grew up, one is led to Moravia on the eastern border of Slovakia. There we visited the city of Trencin, a site that got its start when Roman legions camped there in the centuries before Christ's birth. One can still read the ancient information and "graffiti" they carved in a large rock there.

Since World War II, people have been moved around within Czechoslovakia by a variety of forces. Even before the war was over, the Soviets had begun to demand that farmers give all of their produce to the Army. In return, the Soviets would give them flour and other food to keep them alive. This did not strike the farmers as a very good deal, so many of them abandoned their farms and moved to the city. When the Soviet-backed Czech Communists took over after the war, they began a "collectivization" program which forcibly moved the remaining farmers into centrally organized communes. All of the privately owned land was taken over and merged to create large fields for the new communes. Any sense of relationship between the farmers and their land was then lost.

Today, however, with the Communist government finally gone, the Czechs and Slovaks face a different problem: the young people don't want to go into farming because they see it as little more than very hard work. The sense of reward in working one's own land has been lost now for two generations, and it seems it will be very difficult to recapture.

But times are difficult everywhere in the Czech and Slovak economies, not just in agriculture. Many of Agnes's relatives figure that it will take about ten years to get back to something approaching "normal." But they did see some improvement between 1990, right after the "Velvet Revolution," and 1992. Part of the problem in 1990 was that many of the Russians were reluctant to leave Czechoslovakia, because they knew that things were much worse back in Russia.

Many Slovaks, like Agnes's brother, who runs a small grocery store in his garage, are having to learn about business from scratch. There are many one- or two-person businesses – often Mom-and-Pop operations – that are struggling to get the capital they need to make a go of it. They find themselves having to take on loans with short, five-year balloon payments to get the money they need. It's very risky, but they are hoping that things will be better in five years.

In spite of all of the problems and challenges they face, the Slovak people are very friendly. It was enjoyable visiting them, even though I didn't speak the language. However, after 47 years, nothing really looked as Agnes remembered it. I suppose it would be the same for someone returning to Minnesota after being away for nearly half a century. But, as always, people are people wherever and whenever one goes.

In all of our travels, it comes down to one thing for us. Maybe Americans are spoiled by how good we have it, but, having seen the alternatives, Agnes and I agree that there is no place like the United States!

The authors, Agnes and Willard Daluge in 1998.